A Text Book Of

IT IN MANAGEMENT

For
BBA Semester - III
As Per Savitribai Phule Pune University Revised Syllabus
Effective from June 2014

Gautam Bapat
M.C.A.
Asst. Professor, Computer Science & Applications
MITSOM College,
Pune

| IT in Management | ISBN 978-93-5164-167-4 |

Second Edition : February 2016
© : Author

The text of this publication, or any part thereof, should not be reproduced or transmitted in any form or stored in any computer storage system or device for distribution including photocopy, recording, taping or information retrieval system or reproduced on any disc, tape, perforated media or other information storage device etc., without the written permission of Author with whom the rights are reserved. Breach of this condition is liable for legal action.

Every effort has been made to avoid errors or omissions in this publication. In spite of this, errors may have crept in. Any mistake, error or discrepancy so noted and shall be brought to our notice shall be taken care of in the next edition. It is notified that neither the publisher nor the author or seller shall be responsible for any damage or loss of action to any one, of any kind, in any manner, therefrom.

Published By :
NIRALI PRAKASHAN
Abhyudaya Pragati, 1312, Shivaji Nagar
Off J.M. Road, PUNE – 411005
Tel - (020) 25512336/37/39, Fax - (020) 25511379
Email : niralipune@pragationline.com

Printed By :
Repro Knowledgecast Limited,
Thane

☞ **DISTRIBUTION CENTRES**

PUNE
Nirali Prakashan : 119, Budhwar Peth, Jogeshwari Mandir Lane, Pune 411002, Maharashtra
Tel : (020) 2445 2044, 66022708, Fax : (020) 2445 1538
Email : bookorder@pragationline.com, niralilocal@pragationline.com
Nirali Prakashan : S. No. 28/27, Dhyari, Near Pari Company, Pune 411041
Tel : (020) 24690204 Fax : (020) 24690316
Email : dhyari@pragationline.com, bookorder@pragationline.com

MUMBAI
Nirali Prakashan : 385, S.V.P. Road, Rasdhara Co-op. Hsg. Society Ltd.,
Girgaum, Mumbai 400004, Maharashtra
Tel : (022) 2385 6339 / 2386 9976, Fax : (022) 2386 9976
Email : niralimumbai@pragationline.com

☞ **DISTRIBUTION BRANCHES**

JALGAON
Nirali Prakashan : 34, V. V. Golani Market, Navi Peth, Jalgaon 425001,
Maharashtra, Tel : (0257) 222 0395, Mob : 94234 91860

KOLHAPUR
Nirali Prakashan : New Mahadvar Road, Kedar Plaza, 1st Floor Opp. IDBI Bank
Kolhapur 416 012, Maharashtra. Mob : 9850046155

NAGPUR
Pratibha Book Distributors : Above Maratha Mandir, Shop No. 3, First Floor,
Rani Jhanshi Square, Sitabuldi, Nagpur 440012, Maharashtra
Tel : (0712) 254 7129

DELHI
Nirali Prakashan : 4593/21, Basement, Aggarwal Lane 15, Ansari Road, Daryaganj
Near Times of India Building, New Delhi 110002
Mob : 08505972553

BENGALURU
Pragati Book House : House No. 1, Sanjeevappa Lane, Avenue Road Cross,
Opp. Rice Church, Bengaluru – 560002.
Tel : (080) 64513344, 64513355,Mob : 9880582331, 9845021552
Email:bharatsavla@yahoo.com

CHENNAI
Pragati Books : 9/1, Montieth Road, Behind Taas Mahal, Egmore,
Chennai 600008 Tamil Nadu, Tel : (044) 6518 3535,
Mob : 94440 01782 / 98450 21552 / 98805 82331,
Email : bharatsavla@yahoo.com

niralipune@pragationline.com | www.pragationline.com
Also find us on www.facebook.com/niralibooks

Preface ...

I take an opportunity to present this book entitled as **"IT in Manehent"** to the students of Third Semester (BBA.). The object of this book is to present the subject matter in a most concise and simple manner. The book is written strictly according to the Revised Syllabus of Savitribai Phule Pune University.

The book has its own unique features. It brings out the subject in a very simple and lucid manner for easy and comprehensive understanding of the basic concepts, its intricacies, procedures and practices. This book will help the readers to have a broader view on IT in Management. The language used in this book is easy and will help students to improve their vocabulary of Technical terms and understand the matter in a better and happier way.

I sincerely thank Shri. Dineshbhai Furia and Shri. Jignesh Furia, the publishers, for the confidence reposed in us and giving us this opportunity to reach out to the students of management studies.

I thank Mr. Amar Salunkhe for his important inputs time to time. Mr. Akbar Shaikh painstakingly attended to all the details to make this book appear good.

I also thank Ms. Chaitali Takale, Mr. Ravindra Walodare, Mr. Mahesh Swami, Mr. Sachin Shinde, Nikunj Joshi, Nilesh Deshmukh, Ashok Bodke, Moshin Sayyed and Nitin Thorat.

I have given our best inputs for this book. Any suggestions towards the improvement of this book and sincere comments are most welcome on niralipune@pragationline.com.

AUTHOR

Syllabus ...

Unit 1 : Managing Hardware and Software Assets [8 L]
- Computer Hardware and Information Technology Infrastructure.
- Categories of Computers and Computer System.
- Types of Software's.
- Managing Hardware and Software Assets.

Unit 2 : Managing Data Resources [6 L]
- Organizing Data in a Traditional File Environment.
- The Database Approach to Data Management.
- Creating a Database Environment.
- Database Trends.

Unit 3 : Networking [12 L]
- Concept, Basic elements of a Communication System,
- Data transmission media, Topologies, LAN, MAN, WAN, Internet.

Current Trends in IT Management:
- Use of Social Networks in Business.
- Use of ICT enabled application in Business.
  (design a case study to understand the requirement of IT infrastructure in management of business)

Unit 4 : The Internet and The New Information Technology Infrastructure [12 L]
- The IT infrastructure for the Digital Firm.
- The Internet : The IT infrastructure for the Digital Firm.
- The World Wide Web.
- Management Issues and Decisions.

Unit 5 : Understanding the Business values of System and Managing Change [10 L]
- Understanding the Business Values of Information System.
- The Importance of Change Management in Information System Success and Failure.
- Managing Implementations.

■■■

Contents ...

1. **Managing Hardware and Software Assets**   1.1 – 1.42

2. **Managing Data Resources**   2.1 – 2.30

3. **Networking**   3.1 – 3.28

4. **The Internet and the New Information Technology Infrastructure**   4.1 – 4.52

5. **Understanding the Business Values of System and Managing Change**   5.1 – 5.30

University Question Paper - April 2015, November 2015   P.1 – P.2

Chapter 1...
Managing Hardware and Software Assets

Contents ...

1.1 Introduction to Computer
    1.1.1 What is Computer?
    1.1.2 Definition
    1.1.3 Characteristics
    1.1.4 Computer Generations
    1.1.5 Computer Components
    1.1.6 Types of Computers
    1.1.7 Advantages
    1.1.8 Disadvantages
    1.1.9 Applications
1.2 Computer System Hardware
1.3 Computer Memory
    1.3.1 Primary Memory
        1.3.1.1 RAM
        1.3.1.2 ROM
    1.3.2 Secondary Memory
1.4 Managing Hardware and Software Assets
    1.4.1 Software
    1.4.2 Hardware

1.1 Introduction to Computer

- Now-a-days, computers are the integral part of our lives. Computers are used for the reservation of tickets for airplanes and railways, payment of telephone and electricity bills, deposit and withdrawal of money from banks, processing of business data, forecasting of weather conditions, diagnosis of diseases, searching for information on the Internet, etc.

- Computers are also used extensively in schools, universities, organizations, music industry, movie industry, scientific research, law firms, fashion industry, etc.
- The term computer is derived from the word compute. The word compute means to calculate.
- A computer is an electronic machine that accepts data from the user, processes the data by performing calculations and operations on it, and generates the desired output results.
- Computer performs both simple and complex operations, with speed and accuracy.
- A computer is a general purpose device that can be programmed to carry out a finite set of arithmetic or logical operations.
- A computer is an electronic device that manipulates information, or data. Computer has the ability to store, retrieve, and process data.
- A computer is a programmable machine. The two **principle characteristics of a computer** are:
    1. It responds to a specific set of instructions in a well-defined manner, and
    2. It can execute a prerecorded list of instructions (a program).

1.1.1 What is Computer?

- A computer is an advanced electronic device that takes raw data as input from the user and processes these data under the control of set of instructions (called program) and gives the result (output) and saves output for the future use.
- A computer can process both numerical and non-numerical (arithmetic and logical) calculations.
- A computer works in three stages:
    1. **Input (Data):** Input is the raw data entered into a computer from the input devices. It is the collection of letters, numbers, images etc.
    2. **Process:** Process is the operation performed on data as per given instruction. It is totally internal process of the computer system.
    3. **Output and Storage:** Output is the processed data (information) given by computer after data processing. Output is also called as Result. We can save these results in the storage devices for the future use.

1.1.2 Definition

- A computer is a programmable machine that can store, retrieve, and process data.

OR

- Computer is an electronic machine made up of various electronic devices (parts) to process data.

OR

- Computer is an electronic data processing device which does the: accept and store an input data, process the data input and Output the processed data in required format.

1.1.3 Characteristics

- The main characteristics (capabilities) of computer, which make them powerful and useful are:
    1. **Speed:** Computers are of high speed in its operation. The speed is measured in terms of Instructions Per Second (IPS). All modern computers can process information at a speed of a couple of Million Instructions Per Second (MIPS).
    2. **Accuracy:** Computers are highly accurate in arithmetic operations. They either give correct answer or do not answer at all. Errors can occur in computers but these are mainly due to human rather than technological weakness.
    3. **Reliability:** It is the ability of a computer to perform the same job exactly in the same way for any numbers of times.
    4. **Diligence:** A computer is free from monotony, tiredness, lack of concentration, etc. It can work for hours together without creating any error. If ten million calculations have to be performed, the computer can perform the ten millionth calculation with exactly the same accuracy and speed as the first one.
    5. **Power of Remembering:** Computers can store and recall any amount of information because of its secondary storage capability.
    6. **Integrity:** It is the ability of a computer to carry out a sequence of instructions.
    7. **Versatility:** A computer is capable of performing almost any task provided that the task can be reduced to a series of logical steps.
    8. **No Feelings:** Computers are devoid of emotions. They have no feeling because they are machines.

1.1.4 Computer Generations

- A generation in computer talk is a step in technology. Computers developed after ENIAC have been classified into five generations depending upon the technology used, processing techniques, computer languages, memory systems, I/O devices used etc.
- Following are the main five generations of computers:
    1. **First Generation:** The period of first generation is 1942-1955, (Vacuum tube based).
    2. **Second Generation:** The period of second generation is 1955-1964, (Transistor based).
    3. **Third Generation:** The period of third generation is 1964-1975, (Integrated Circuit based).
    4. **Fourth Generation:** The period of fourth generation is 1975-1989, (VLSI microprocessor based).
    5. **Fifth Generation:** The period of fifth generation is 1989-onwards, (ULSI microprocessor based).

1. **First Generation Computers (1942-1955):**
   - The first generation computers used Vacuum Tubes and machine languages were used for giving instructions. The computer of this generation was very large in size and their programming was a difficult task.
   - The first commercial electronic digital computer capable of using stored programs was called "Universal Automatic Calculator" (UNIVAC) built by Macuchy and Eckert in 1951. Punched cards were used for feeding and retrieving of information.
   - The major first generation computers are UNIVAC -1, IBM -701, IBM -650, ENIAC, EDVAC, EDSAC, etc.
   - These computers were the fastest calculating devices of their time. They could perform computations in milliseconds. Vacuum tube technology made possible the advent of electronic digital computers.
   - The limitations of this generation computers are slow in operating speed, restricted computing capacity, very large space requirement, non-portability, etc.

2. **Second Generation Computers (1955-1964):**
   - Computers are entered into second generation by the introduction of Transistors. Vacuum tubes were replaced by tiny solid-state components called transistors.
   - Transistors were highly reliable, require less power and are faster than vacuum tubes. High Level Languages such as FORTRAN, COBOL, ALGOL etc. were introduced. The practice of writing programs in Machine languages were replaced by High Level Languages. Punched cards were used for input-output operations.
   - Major second generation computers are IBM -1400 series, 7000 series, Honeywell 200, etc.
   - The advantages of second-generation computers are:
     (i) Smaller in size as compared to first generation.
     (ii) More reliable, less prone to hardware failures.
     (iii) Less heat generation.
     (iv) Faster than a first generation computers, computational time is in microseconds.
     (v) Better portability.
     (vi) Easier to program and use.

3. **Third Generation Computers (1964-1975):**
   - The third generation computers used the new technology, Integrated Circuits (IC) intented by Jack and Noyce in 1958. All electronic components like transistors, resistors and capacitors were fabricated on silicon chips.
   - Computers were designed by making use of ICs. IC has higher speed, larger storage capacity and smaller size.

- Operating systems were introduced for use in computers. Significant advances in hardware technology made the introduction of keyboards and monitors for data input and output. More high level languages like Pascal, RPG were also introduced.
- Major third generation computers are IBM-360 series, ICL-1900 series, CDC's CYBER-175, etc.
- The advantages of third generation computers are:
    (i) Smaller in size as compared to previous generation computers.
    (ii) More reliable than second generation.
    (iii) Computational time is in nanoseconds.
    (iv) Maintenance cost is low.
    (v) Easily portable.
    (vi) Time sharing OS (Operating System) allowed interactive and simultaneous use of systems.
    (vii) Minicomputers made computers affordable to small companies.

4. The Fourth Generation Computers (1975-1989):
- The ICs used in third generation computers had about 10 to 100 transistors per unit. This technology was called Small-Scale Integration (SSI).
- Later, with the advancement of technology for manufacturing ICs, it is possible to integrate 10,000 transistors in a single IC. This technology is called Large-Scale Integration (LSI).
- Very Large Scale Integration (VLSI) can pack a million or more transistors on a single chip. LSI and VLSI technologies led to the introduction of Microprocessors.
- Computers which are designed using Microprocessors become the fourth generation computers. Magnetic disks become the primary means for external storage.
- Intel introduced the first microprocessor 4004 using LSI. The languages C, LISP, Prolog become popular. Present day computers are fourth generation computers.
- Major fourth generation computers are IBM System 370, CRAY –MPC, WIPRO 860, IBM AS/400/B60, IBM ps/2 MODEL 80, HCL Magnum, etc.
- The main advantages of fourth generation computers are:
    (i) Smallest in size.
    (ii) Very reliable.
    (iii) Heat generated is negligible.
    (iv) Very fast in computation.
    (v) Easily portable.
    (vi) GUI enabled users to quickly learn how to use computer.
    (vii) General purpose computer.
    (viii) Low cost.

5. Fifth Generation Computers (1989 onwards):

- Fifth generation computers are capable of parallel processing, high speed computing and artificial intelligence.
- They have an architecture which allows more neural problem solving ability. These machines use the principle of Artificial Intelligence (AI).
- They have the ability to understand natural languages like English, Malayalam, etc., thus they can converse with human beings. Computer languages such as LISP, PROLOG, C, C++, etc., are available to program such computers.
- Some computer types of this generation are Desktop, Laptop, NoteBook etc.

1.1.5 Computer Components

- Fig. 1.1 shows block diagram of a computer with its various components.

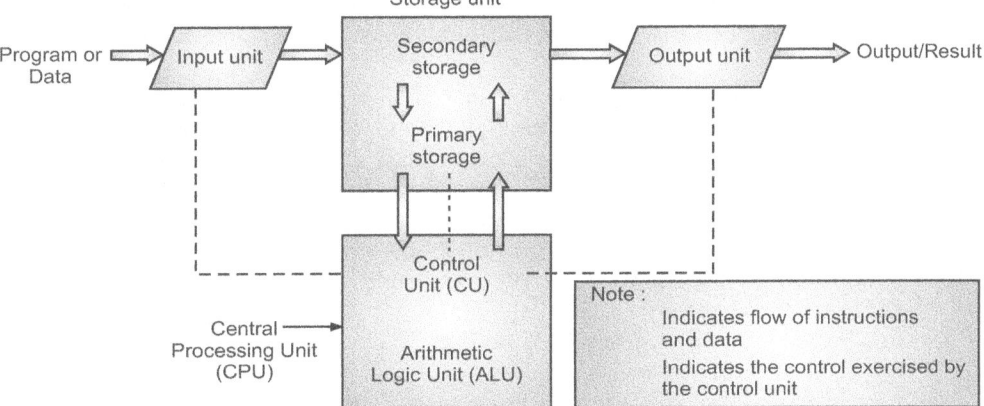

Fig. 1.1: Basic organisation of computer system

- A computer mainly consists of three units:

1. Input Unit:
- Input unit is used for entering data into the computer. Input unit contains devices with the help of which we enter data into computer.
- Input unit makes link between user and computer. The input devices translate the human readable information into the form understandable by computer i.e. in binary with the help of input interfaces.
- Some important input devices which are used in computer systems are Keyboard, Mouse, Joystick, Light pen, Trackball, Scanner, Graphic tablet, Microphone, Magnetic Ink Card Reader (MICR), Optical Character Reader (OCR), Bar Code Reader, Optical Mark Reader (OMR) and so on.

- An input device performs the following functions:
    (i) It accepts (i.e. reads) the list of instruction and data from the user.
    (ii) It converts these instructions and data in binary form which is understood by the computer.
    (iii) It supplies the converted instructions and data to the computer for further processing.

2. **Process Unit:**
- The task of performing operations like arithmetic and logical operations is called processing.
- The Central Processing Unit (CPU) takes data and instructions from the storage unit and makes all sorts of calculations based on the instructions given and the type of data provided. It is then sent back to the storage unit.
- CPU is the heart of every computer system that performs the user instructions.
- CPU itself has three components and ALU (Arithmetic Logic Unit), Memory Unit and Control Unit.

    (i) Arithmetic Logical Unit (ALU): This unit is responsible for arithmetic and logical operations. After you enter data through the input device it is stored in the primary storage unit. The actual processing of the data and instruction are performed by Arithmetic Logical Unit. The major operations performed by the ALU are addition, subtraction, multiplication, division, logic and comparison.

    (ii) CU (Control Unit): This unit is responsible for program execution, fetching information from memory, decoding it and sending it at appropriate place in the computer to execute it.

    CU unit controls the operations of all parts of computer. It does not carry out any actual data processing operations.

    Functions of control unit are:
    1. It obtains the instructions from the memory, interprets them and directs the operation of the computer.
    2. It is responsible for controlling the transfer of data and instructions among other units of a computer.
    3. It communicates with Input/Output devices for transfer of data or results from storage.
    4. It does not process or store data.
    5. It manages and coordinates all the other units of the computer.

    (iii) Memory or Storage Unit: The process of saving data and instruction permanently or temporally is known as storage. This unit can store instruction, data and intermediate results. This unit supplies information to the other units of the computer when needed. It is also known as internal storage unit or main memory or primary storage or Random Access Memory (RAM). Its size affects speed, power and capability.

There are two types of memories in the computer: primary memory (storage) like RAM and secondary memory (storage) like ROM.

Storage unit provides space for storing data and instructions.

Functions of memory unit are:
1. It stores intermediate results of processing.
2. All inputs and outputs are transmitted through main memory.
3. It stores all the data to be processed and the instructions required for processing.
4. It stores final results of processing before these results are released to an output device.

3. Output Unit:
- The result of computer processing is called as output. This result is communicated to user through a device called output device.
- Output unit consists of devices with the help of which we get the information from computer. This unit is a link between computer and users.
- Output devices translate the computer's output into the form understandable by user.
- Some important output devices which are used in computer systems are Monitors, Plotter, Printer and so on.
- The following functions are performed by an output device:
    (i) It accepts results produced by the computer which are in binary coded form and hence cannot be understood by us. e.g. suppose we want to add the results of products A B.
    (ii) It converts coded results to human readable form.
    (iii) It supplies the converted form to the user through devices.

1.1.6 Types of Computers
- Computers can be classified based on their principles of operation or on their configuration. By configuration, we mean the size, speed of performing computation and storage capacity of a computer.

1. Types of Computers based on Principles of Operation:
- There are three different types of computers according to the principles of operation. These three types of computers are shown in Fig. 1.2.

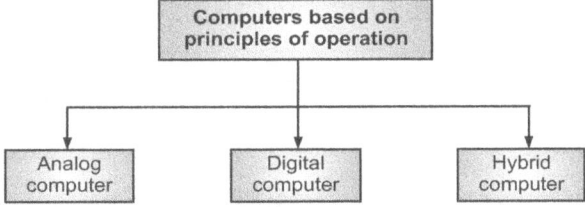

Fig. 1.2: Types of computers based on operation

(i) Analog Computers:
- Analog computer is a computing device that works on continuous range of values. The results given by the analog computers will only be approximate since they deal with quantities that vary continuously.
- Analog computers generally deal with physical variables such as voltage, pressure, temperature, speed, etc.

(ii) Digital Computers:
- A digital computer operates on digital data such as numbers. It uses binary number system in which there are only two digits 0 and 1. Each one is called a bit.
- The digital computer is designed using digital circuits in which there are two levels for an input or output signal. These two levels are known as logic 0 and logic 1. Digital Computers can give more accurate and faster results.
- Digital computer is well suited for solving complex problems in engineering and technology. Hence digital computers have an increasing use in the field of design, research and data processing.
- Based on the purpose, Digital computers can be further classified as,
    - **(a) General Purpose Computers:** General purpose computers are used for any type of applications. They can store different programs and do the jobs as per the instructions specified on those programs. Most of the computers that we see today, are general purpose computers.
    - **(b) Special Purpose Computers:** Special purpose computer is one that is built for a specific application.

(iii) Hybrid Computers:
- A hybrid computer combines the desirable features of analog and digital computers.
- Hybrid COMPUTER is mostly used for automatic operations of complicated physical processes and machines.
- Now-a-days analog-to-digital and digital-to-analog converters are used for transforming the data into suitable form for either type of computation.

2. Types of Computers based on Configuration:
- There are four different types of computers based on their performance and capacity.
- These four types are shown in Fig. 1.3.

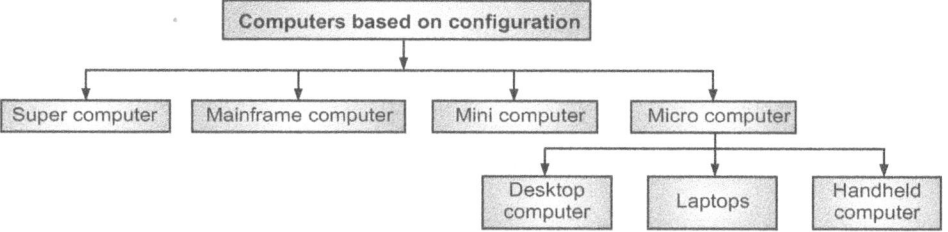

Fig. 1.3: Types of computer according to configuration

(i) Super Computers:

- Super computers are one of the fastest computers currently available.
- Supercomputers are very expensive and are employed for specialized applications that require immense amounts of mathematical calculations (number crunching). For example, weather forecasting , scientific simulations, (animated) graphics, fluid dynamic calculations, nuclear energy research, electronic design, and analysis of geological data (for example, in petrochemical prospecting).
- These computers can process billions of instructions per second. Normally, they will be used for applications which require intensive numerical computations such as stock analysis, weather forecasting etc.
- Super computers has very high storage capacity and it support parallel processing.
- As of July 2009, the IBM Roadrunner, located at Los Alamos National Laboratory, is the fastest super computer in the world.

Fig. 1.4: Super computer

(ii) Mainframe Computers:

- Mainframe computers can also process data at very high speeds i.e., hundreds of million instructions per second and they are also quite expensive.
- Normally, they are used in critical and complex applications and complex like banking, airlines and railways etc.
- Mainframe is a very large in size and is an expensive computer capable of supporting hundreds, or even thousands, of users simultaneously.
- Mainframe executes many programs concurrently.
- Mainframe has high storage capacity and it support parallel processing.

Fig. 1.5: Mainframe computer

(iii) Mini Computers:

- Mini computers are faster than the micro computer with access to more storage space and more I/O devices, the mini computer is used when large groups need to data access simultaneously.
- Mini computers are designed for single user.
- Mini computers are lower to mainframe computers in terms of speed and storage capacity.
- They are also less expensive than mainframe computers. Some of the features of mainframes will not be available in mini computers. Hence, their performance is less than that of mainframes.

Fig. 1.6: Mini computer

(iv) Micro Computers:

- The invention of microprocessor (single chip CPU) gave birth to the much cheaper micro-computers.
- The micro computer is also known as Personal Computer (PC).
- A PC can be defined as a small, relatively inexpensive computer designed for an individual user.
- PCs are based on the microprocessor technology that enables manufacturers to put an entire CPU on one chip. Businesses use personal computers for word processing, accounting, desktop publishing, and for running spreadsheet and database management applications.
- At home, the most popular use for personal computers is for playing games and surfing the Internet.
- They are further classified into following categories:

(a) Desktop Computers:

- Today the Desktop computers are the most popular computer systems. Desktop computers are also known as Personal Computers or simply PCs.
- They are usually easier to use and more affordable. They are normally intended for individual users for their word processing and other small application requirements.

Fig. 1.7: Desktop computer

(b) Laptop Computers:

- Laptop computers are portable computers just like a briefcase.
- Laptops are lightweight computers with a thin screen.
- Laptops are also called as notebook computers because of their small size.
- Laptops can operate on batteries and hence are very popular with travellers. The screen folds down onto the keyboard when not in use.

Fig. 1.8: Laptops

(c) Handheld Computers:

- Handheld computers are small portable computers designed to be held in one hand (See Fig. 1.9).
- Handheld computers or Personal Digital Assistants (PDAs) are pen-based and also battery-powered.

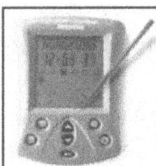

Fig. 1.9: Handheld computers

- PDAs are small and can be carried anywhere. They use a pen like stylus and accept handwritten input directly on the screen.
- PDAs are not as powerful as desktops or laptops but they are used for scheduling appointments, storing addresses and playing games.
- PDAs have touch screens which we use with a finger or a stylus.

1.1.7 Advantages

1. **High Speed:** Computer is a very fast device. Computer can perform millions of calculations in a few seconds as compared to man who can spend many months for doing the same task.
2. **Accuracy:** Computer are very accurate. The computer has performed calculations 100% error free.
3. **Storage Capability:** Computers can store large amount of data. Computers can store any type of data such as images, videos, text, audio and any other type.
4. **Diligence:** Unlike human beings, a computer is free from monotony, tiredness and lack of concentration. Computers can work continuously without creating any error and boredom and it can do repeated work with same speed and accuracy.
5. **Automation:** Computer is a automatic machine and automation means ability to perform the task automatically. Once, a program is given to computer i.e. stored in computer memory, the program and instruction can control the program execution without human interaction.
6. **Reduction in Paper Work:** The use of computers for data processing in an organization leads to reduction in paper work and speeds up the process.
7. **Reduction in Cost:** Though the initial investment for installing a computer is high but it substantially reduces the cost of each of its transaction.
8. **Reliability:** A computer is a reliable machine and modern electronic components have failure free long lives. Computers are designed to make maintenance easy and simple.
9. **Versatility:** A computer is a very versatile machine and is very flexible in performing the jobs to be done. Computer can be used to solve the problems relating to various different fields. At one instant, it may be solving a complex scientific problem and the very next moment it may be playing a card game.

1.1.8 Disadvantages

1. **No Intelligence:** A computer is a machine and has no intelligence of its own to perform any task. Each and every instruction has to be given to computer. A computer can not take any decision on its own.
2. **Environment:** The operating environment of computer should be dust free and suitable to it.
3. **No Feeling:** Computer has no feeling or emotions. So it cannot make Judgement based on feeling, taste, experience and knowledge unlike a human being.
4. **Dependency:** Computers can perform function as instructed by user and so it is fully dependent on human being.

1.1.9 Applications

1. **Business:** The computer's characteristic as high speed of calculation, diligence, accuracy, reliability, or versatility has made it an integrated part in all business organisations. Computers are used in business organisation like: Payroll Calculations, Budgeting, Sales Analysis, Financial forecasting, Managing employees database Maintenance of stocks and so on.

2. **Insurance:** Insurance companies are keeping all records up to date with the help of computer. The Insurance Companies, Finance houses and Stock broking firms are widely using computers for their concerns. Insurance companies are maintaining a database of all clients with information showing: how to continue with policies, starting date of the policies, next due installment of a policy, maturity date, interests due, survival benefits, bonus and so on.

3. **Banking:** Today Banking is almost dependent on computer. Banks provide facilities like on-line accounting facility, which include current balances, deposits, overdrafts, interest charges, shares and trustee records. ATM machines are making it even easier for customers to deal with banks.

4. **Health Care:** Today, computers have become important part in all medical systems. The computers are being used in hospitals to keep the record of patients and medicines. Computers are also used in scanning and diagnosing different diseases. ECG, EEG, Ultrasounds and CT Scans etc. are also done by computerised machines. Some of major fields of health care in which computer are used:

    (i) **Diagnostic System:** Computers are used to collect data and identify cause of illness.

    (ii) **Lab-diagnostic System:** All tests can be done and reports are prepared by computer.

    (iii) **Patient Monitoring System:** These are used to check patient's signs for abnormality such as in Cardiac Arrest, ECG etc.

    (iv) **Pharma Information System:** Computer checks Drug-Labels, Expiry dates, harmful drug side effects etc.

    (v) Nowadays, computers are also used in **performing surgery**.

5. **Engineering Design:** Computers are widely used in Engineering purposes like CAD (Computer Aided Design). Some fields used in computers are:

    (i) **Industrial Engineering:** Computers deals with design, implementation and improvement of Integrated systems of people, materials and equipments.

    (ii) **Architectural Engineering:** Computers help in planning towns, designing buildings, determining a range of buildings on a site using both 2D and 3D drawings.

    (iii) **Structural Engineering:** Requires stress and strain analysis required for design of Ships, Buildings, Budgets, Airplanes etc.

6. **Communication:** Communication means to convey a message, an idea, a picture or speech that is received and understood clearly and correctly by the person for whom it is meant. Some main areas in this category are E-mail, Chatting, FTP, Telnet, Video-conferencing etc.
7. **Education:** The computer has provided a lot of facilities in the education system like:
   (i) It is used to prepare a database about student performance and analysis is carried out.
   (ii) The uses of computer provide a tool in the Education system is known as CBE (Computer Based Education).
   (iii) The computer education is very familiar and rapidly increasing the graph of computer students.
   (iv) CBE involves Control, Delivery and Evaluation of learning.
   (v) There are number of methods in which educational institutions can use computer to educate the students.
8. **Marketing:** In marketing uses of computer are:
   (i) **At Home Shopping:** At home shopping has been made possible through use of computerised catalogues that provide access to product information and permit direct entry of orders to be filled by the customers.
   (ii) **Advertising:** With computers, advertising professionals create art and graphics, write and revise copy, and print and disseminate ads with the goal of selling more products.
9. **Military:** Computers are largely used in defence. Today's modern tanks, missiles, weapons etc. employ computerised control systems. Some military areas where a computer has been used are Missile control, Military communication, Military operation and planning, Smart weapons and so on.
10. **Government Applications:** Computers play an important role in government applications. Some major fields in this category are Budgets, Sales tax department, Income tax department, Male/Female ratio, Computerization of voters lists, Computerization of Driving Licensing system, Computerization of PAN card, Weather Forecasting and so on.

1.2 Computer System Hardware

- The actual physical components that constitute a computer are known as Computer Hardware.
- In other words, anything in the computer that you can touch and see is the hardware. For example, CPU, monitor, keyboard, ICs, resistors, etc.
- Hardware represents the physical and tangible components of the computer i.e. the components that can be seen and touched.

- Examples of hardware:
    1. **Input devices:** keyboard, mouse, scanners, tight pen etc.
    2. **Output devices:** printer, monitor etc.
    3. **Secondary storage devices:** Hard disk, CD, DVD, floppy etc.
    4. **Internal components:** CPU, motherboard, RAM etc.
- Fig. 1.10 shows common hardware parts of computer system.

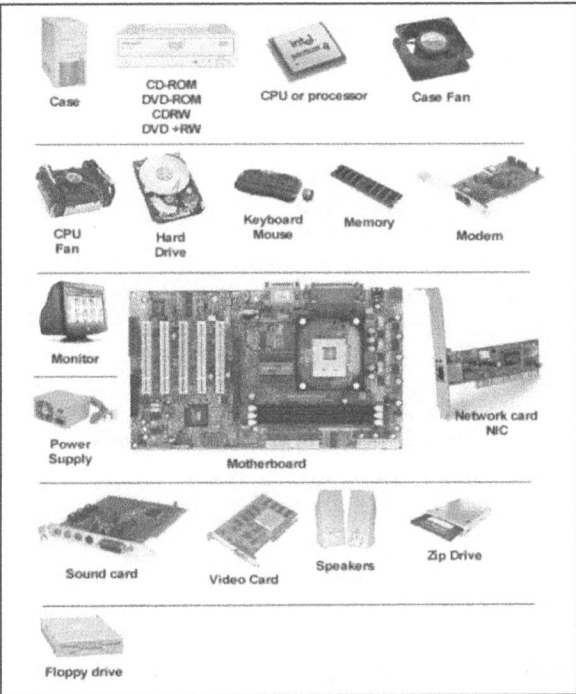

Fig. 1.10: Various hardware parts of a computer

1.3 Computer Memory

- Basically, memory is a means for storing data or information in the form of binary words.
- Memory is made up of storage locations in which numeric or alphanumeric information or programs (sets of instructions that a computer executes to achieve a desired result) may be stored.
- The main function of memory is to store the data or information.
- Computer data storage, often called storage or memory, is a technology consisting of computer components and recording media used to retain digital data.

- A memory is just like a human brain. It is used to store data and instruction.
- Computer memory is the storage space in computer where data is to be processed and instructions required for processing are stored.
- The memory is divided into large number of small parts. Each part is called cell. Each location or cell has a unique address which varies from zero to memory size minus one.

Definition:
- The memory used to store data is called data memory, and the memory used to store programmes is called program memory. The sub-system of a digital processing system which provides the storage facility is called memory.
- Fig. 1.11 shows classification of memories:

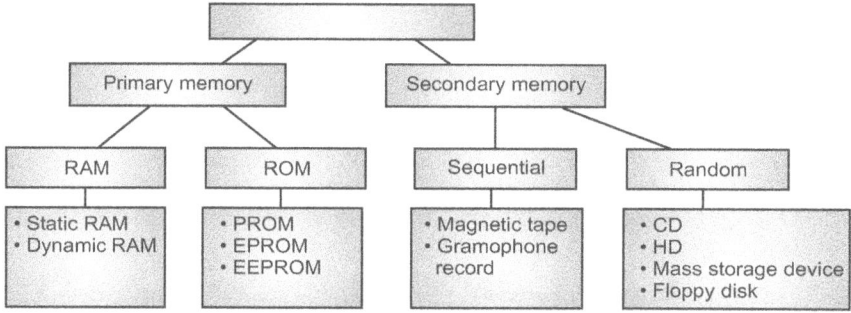

Fig. 1.11: Classification of memories

- There are mainly two types of computer memory i.e. primary ands secondary memory discussed below.

1.3.1 Primary Memory

- Primary memory is also called as main memory or primary storage or internal memory.
- Primary memory often referred to simply as memory is the only one directly accessible to the CPU.
- The CPU continuously reads instructions stored, there and executes them as required. Any data actively operated on is also stored there is uniform manner.
- Primary memories are generally a part of a system, that are used to functonate system.
- These memories help the system to store intermediate data or gas some specific data as instructions that are necessary to make system run.
- Primary memory holds only those data and instructions on which computer is currently working. It has limited capacity and data get lost when power is switched OFF.
- Primary memory is generally made up of semiconductor device. These memories are not as fast as registers. The data and instruction required to be processed earlier reside in main memory. It is divided into two subcategories RAM and ROM.

Characteristics of main memory:
(i) These are semiconductor memories.
(ii) Usually volatile memory. Data is lost in case power is switch off.
(iii) It is working memory of the computer.
(iv) Faster than secondary memories.
(v) A computer cannot run without primary memory.

Fig. 1.12

Advantages and Disadvantages of Primary Storage (Memory):
1. Primary storage is closer to the CPU and/or is integrated onto it and therefore it is faster.
2. All primary storage is temporary.
3. Primary storage is smaller in capacity.
4. Primary storage is usually faster therefore, it is more expensive.

1.3.1.1 RAM

- A RAM constitutes the internal memory of the CPU for storing data, program and program result.
- RAM is read/write memory. It is called Random Access Memory (RAM).
- RAM is volatile, i.e. data stored in it is lost when we switch off the computer or if there is a power failure. Hence a backup Uninterruptible Power System (UPS) is often used with computers. RAM is small, both in terms of its physical size and in the amount of data it can hold.
- This memory is accessible from any memory location anytime. One can switch to one place to another place in memory randomly.
- RAM is of two types i.e. Static RAM (SRAM) and Dynamic RAM (DRAM).

1. SRAM (Static Random Access Memory):
- SRAM is a type of semiconductor memory where the word static indicates that, it does not need to be periodically refreshed, as SRAM uses bistable latching circuitry to store each bit.
- SRAM is volatile in the conventional sense that data is eventually lost when the memory is not powered.
- Static RAM is used as cache memory needs to be very fast and small.

Characteristics of the Static RAM:
   (a) There is no need to refresh.
   (b) Used as cache memory.
   (c) It has long data lifetime.
   (d) High power consumption.
   (e) Faster.
   (f) Large size.
   (g) Expensive.

2. **DRAM (Dynamic Random Access Memory):**
- DRAM is a type of random access memory that stores each bit of data in a separate capacitor within an integrated circuit. Since real capacitors leak charge, the information eventually fades unless the capacitor charge is refreshed periodically. Because of this refresh requirement, it is a dynamic memory as opposed to SRAM and other static memory.

Characteristics of the Dynamic RAM:
   (h) Need to refresh continuously.
   (i) Used as RAM.
   (j) It has short data lifetime.
   (k) Less power consumption.
   (l) Slower as compared to SRAM.
   (m) lesser in size.
   (n) Less expensive.

1.3.1.2 ROM

- ROM stands for Read Only Memory.
- The memory from which we can only read but cannot write on it.
- This type of memory is non-volatile. The information is stored permanently in such memories during manufacture.
- ROM also known as **firmware**, is an integrated circuit programmed with specific data when it is manufactured.
- A ROM, stores such instruction as are required to start computer when electricity is first turned on, this operation is referred to as bootstrap.
- ROM chip are not only used in the computer but also in other electronic items like washing machine and microwave oven.
- Various types of ROM are given below:
    1. **MROM (Masked ROM):** The very first ROMs were hard-wired devices that contained a pre-programmed set of data or instructions. These kind of ROMs are known as masked ROMs. It is an inexpensive ROM.

2. **PROM (Programmable Read Only Memory):** PROM is read-only memory that can be modified only once by a user. The user buys a blank PROM and enters the desired contents using a PROM programmer. Inside the PROM chip there are small fuses which are burnt open during programming. It can be programmed only once and is not erasable.

   A Programmable Read-Only Memory or Field Programmable Read-Only Memory (FPROM) is a form of digital memory where the setting of each bit is locked by a fuse or antifuse.

3. **EPROM (Erasable and Programmable Read Only Memory):** An EPROM is a type of memory chip that retains its data when its power supply is switched-OFF. The EPROM can be erased by exposing it to ultra-violet light for a duration of up to 40 minutes. Usually, a EPROM eraser achieves this function. During programming an electrical charge is trapped in an insulated gate region. The charge is retained for more than ten years because the charge has no leakage path. For erasing this charge, ultra-violet light is passed through a quartz crystal window (lid). This exposure to ultra-violet light dissipates the charge. During normal use the quartz lid is sealed with a sticker.

4. **EEPROM (Electrically Erasable and Programmable Read Only Memory):** EEPROM (also written as E^2PROM). EEPROM is a type of non-volatile memory used in computers and other electronic devices to store small amounts of data that must be saved when power is removed. The EEPROM is programmed and erased electrically. It can be erased and reprogrammed about ten thousand times. Both erasing and programming take about 4 to 10 ms (millisecond). In EEPROM, any location can be selectively erased and programmed. EEPROMs can be erased one byte at a time, rather than erasing the entire chip. Hence, the process of re-programming is flexible but slow.

Advantages of ROM:
1. Cheaper than RAMs.
2. Non-volatile in nature.
3. More Reliable than RAMs.
4. Its contents are always known and can be verified.
5. Easy and simple to test.
6. These can not be accidentally changed.
7. These are static and do not require refreshing.

Difference between RAM and ROM:

RAM	ROM
1. RAM stands for Random Access Memory.	1. ROM stands for Read Only Memory.
2. It is temporary memory.	2. It is permanent memory.
3. It is volatile memory.	3. It is non-volatile memory.
4. Information stored by user.	4. Information stored by manufacturer.
5. Read/write operations can be performed.	5. Only read can be performed.
6. Every location can be visited directly or randomly.	6. Longer access time.
7. It stores data, program instructions during program execution.	7. It stores system software programs for basic operations.

1.3.2 Secondary Memory

- Secondary storage (also known as external memory or auxiliary storage or permanent storage) differs from primary storage in that it is not directly accessible by the CPU.
- The computer usually uses its input/output channels to access secondary storage and transfers the desired data using intermediate area in primary storage.
- Secondary storage does not lose the data when the device is powered down it is non-volatile.
- Secondary memories are abstract from any system like one can carry this memory any where. A data is permanently stored in this types of memories for long period.
- This type of memory is also known as external memory. It is slower than main memory.
- These are used for storing Data/Information permanently.
- CPU directly does not access these memories instead they are accessed via input-output routines. Contents of secondary memories are first transferred to main memory, and then CPU can access it. For example: disk, CD-ROM, DVD etc.

Characteristic of Secondary Memory:
1. These are magnetic and optical memories.
2. It is used for storage of the data in the computer.
3. Slower than primary memories.
4. It is non-volatile memory i.e. data is permanently stored even if power is switched off.
5. It is known as backup memory.
6. Computer may run without secondary memory.

Advantages and Disadvantages of Secondary Memory:
1. All secondary storage is permanent.
2. Secondary storage is closer to the CPU via cables and therefore is slower.
3. Secondary storage has bigger capacity.
4. Secondary storage is usually cheaper and large.

Types of Secondary Memory:

1. Magnetic Tape:
- The magnetic tape is similar to the audio tape recorder.
- Magnetic tape is a recording medium consisting of a thin tape with a coating of a fine magnetic material, used for recording analog or digital data.
- A device that stores computer data on magnetic tape is a tape drive. The capacity of tape media are generally on the same order as hard disk drives.
- Magnetic tapes generally transfer data a bit slower than hard drives, however magnetic tapes are cheaper and are more durable.
- Fig. 1.13 shows magnetic tape.

Fig. 1.13: Magnetic tape

2. Floppy Disk:
- Floppy Disks are the ubiquitous form of data storage between 1980's and early 2000's.
- However, they have now been superseded by data storage methods with much greater capacity, such as USB flash drives. Floppy disks comes in 3 sizes: 8-inches, 5.5-inches and 3.5-inches.
- The capacities of Floppy disks vary between 1-250 Megabytes and these devices were very slow, reading data at rates of bytes and kbytes/second. However, most are very small and portable.
- Fig. 1.14 shows floppy disk.

Fig. 1.14: Floppy

3. Hard Disk:
- The hard disk drive is the main and usually largest data storage device in a computer. It is a non-volatile, random access digital magnetic data storage device.
- A hard drive is made up of platters which stored the data, and read/write heads to transfer data.
- A Hard Drive is generally the fastest of the secondary storage devices, and has the largest data storage capacity, approximately the same as magnetic tapes.

IT in Management   **Managing Hardware and Software Assets**

- Hard drives however, are not very portable and are primarily used internally in a computer system. Some people use hard drives externally as a form of storage and as a substitute for portable storage, hard drives used for these purposes are called external hard drives.
- A hard disk is divided into tracks and sectors. Data on this hard disk is positioned into these tracks and sectors so they can be easily read by the heads and also to help reduce fragmentation on the hard disk.
- Fig. 1.16 depicting how a hard disk is divided into tracks and sectors while Fig. 1.15 shows hard disk.

Fig. 1.15: HDD Hard disk drive

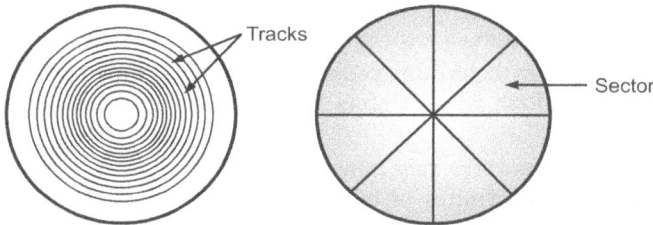

Fig. 1.16: Hard disk tracks and sectors

4. Optical Disks:

- Optical disk is an electronic data storage medium from which data is read and written to by using a low-powered laser beam.
- Optical disks are flat, circular, plastic or glass disk on which data is stored in the form of light and dark pits.
- There are three basic types of optical disks i.e. Read-only optical disks, Write once read many Optical disks and Rewritable Optical disks.
- Two main types of optical disks are:
  - **(i) CD:** CD is an abbreviation of Compact Disk. CD is a form of data storage that can transfer data up to the speed of 7800 KB/s. A standard 120 mm CD holds up to 700 MB of data, or about 70 minutes of audio. There are two types of CD: CD-ROM and CD-RW, CD-ROM are stands for CD-Read Only Memory and they function the same way Read Only Memory Does. CD-RW Stards for CD-Rewritable, these disks can be erased and rewritten at any time. Fig. 1.17 shows a CD.

Fig. 1.17: CD

(ii) DVD: DVD is an abbreviation of Digital Versatile Disc. DVD is an optical disc storage media format that can be used for data storage. The DVD supports disks with capacities of 4.7 GB to 17 GB and access rates of 600 KBps to 1.3 MBps. A standard DVD disc store up to 4.7 GB of data. There are two types of DVD's: DVD-ROM and DVD-RW. DVD-ROM are stands for DVD-Read Only Memory and they function the same way Read Only Memory Does. DVD-RW stands for DVD-Rewritable, these disks can be erased and rewritten at any time.

Fig. 1.18: DVD

5. **Flash Drive:**
- A flash drive is a small external storage device, typically the size of a human thumb that consists of flash memory.
- USB flash drives are removable and rewritable reads and writes to flash memory. They are a solid-state storage medium that is both inexpensive and durable.
- Currently, USB 2.0 flash drives on the market are able to reach a data transfer speed of 480 Mbps and USB 3.0 has transmission speeds of up to 5 Gbps. USB Flash drives vary in sizes from 8 Megabytes to 512 Gigabytes. More commonly used sizes vary from 2 Gigabytes -16 Gigabytes. Fig. 1.19 shows flash drive.

Fig. 1.19: Flash drives

6. Flash Memory cards:

- Fig. 1.20 (a) shows flash memory card.
- Flash memory is a EEPROM non-volatile computer storage chip. These Memory cards currently vary in sizes between 1 Gigabytes -16 Gigabytes and they transfer data at a rate of approximately 14.65 MB/s.
- Flash memory cards have most of the same characteristics of a flash drive in that they are inexpensive and durable, and are very small. However Flash memory cards are Flat and have a size of about 1 inch * 0.75 inch with a thickness of about 2mm.
- Flash memory cards also have a smaller version which is used within cell phones. (See Fig. 1.20 (b)).
- These smaller cards are about 6mmX3mm in size and are less than 1mm thick.

(a)

(b)

Fig. 1.20: Flash memory card

Difference between Primary and Secondary Storages (Memory):

Primary Storage	Secondary Storage
1. It is a part of CPU.	1. It is not a part of CPU.
2. It is the internal or main memory.	2. It is the external memory and resides on disk.
3. Most primary storage is temporary.	3. All secondary storage is permanent.
4. Primary storage is expensive and smaller.	4. Secondary storage is usually cheaper and large.
5. Primary storage is usually faster.	5. Secondary storage connects to the CPU via cables and therefore is slower.
6. The access time is less a few nanoseconds.	6. The access time is more a few milliseconds.
7. It is a medium capacity memory.	7. It is a high capacity memory.
8. It is further classified as RAM and ROM.	8. There are different types of secondary storage devices such as hard disk, floppy disk, CD-ROM etc.

Cache Memory:
- Cache memory is a very high speed memory placed in between RAM and CPU. Cache memory increases the speed of processing.
- Cache memory is a storage buffer that stores the data that is used more often, temporarily, and makes them available to CPU at a fast rate. During processing, CPU first checks cache for the required data. If data is not found in cache, then it looks in the RAM for data.
- To access the cache memory, CPU does not have to use the motherboard's system bus for data transfer.
- Cache memory is built into the processor, and may also be located next to it on a separate chip between the CPU and RAM. Cache built into the CPU is faster than separate cache, running at the speed of the microprocessor itself. However, separate cache is roughly twice as fast as RAM.

Types of Computer Software
- Designed to store data, a computer is able to function in different and desired ways only due to a number of software applications that empower it.
- Various types of computer software help it execute a variety of operations every day. Computer software is available in different forms and types.

Classification of Computer Software
- Broadly, computer software can be classified into three categories. One, system software is the most important component for running a system or computer. System software is also known as operating system which helps start a computer and works as a main platform in order to run any application. A number of operating systems are in vogue that empower systems globally. However, these operating systems have a category of server and personal computer operating systems.
- One of the most popular operating systems, of course, is Microsoft's Windows OS. Other known names are Linux, iMac, UNIX and DOS, among others. Secondly, application software plays an important part in helping users execute different tasks using computer. It is the name computer programs are designated with. Quite a few known application software are known as word processor and web browser.
- Among the word processors, while all of us have certainly seen or used Microsoft Word or Open Office, etc, web browsers such as Internet Explorer, Firefox, Safari and Chrome, are among others are types of widely used tools that help users to access the Internet. But application software goes a little further with industry specific applications and design tools that help in designing documents or sometimes products with computer-aided design tools. Manufacturing activity, which these tools play a critical role from designing to innovating, is heavily reliant on them.
- The third category constitutes computer programming tools for instance, compilers and linkers. These tools are used to translate and combine computer program source code. This category is at the core of vastly changing software development field.

Enterprise-grade applications
- While system software is at the core of running a computer and putting it to life, it further helps drive operations and has become the lifeline of organizations and governments globally. A number of changes have taken place in computer software in last one century as it has evolved significantly and allows users to multitask, to share/store data on-the-move and improves connectivity between different computers around the globe.
- Living examples of application software that drive businesses, banks and governments on daily-basis are ERP (enterprise resource planning), CRM (customer relationship management) and BI (business intelligence) applications. Thousands of businesses around the world operate seamlessly using ERP and CRM applications. These are heavy-duty software that boast agility and seamless performance in any organization. Enterprises with thousands of employees and millions of customers rely on them for faster delivery of services and reduce leakages in the system.

Customization vs Off-the-shelf software
- In addition, any individual software package, which may fall into any of the above categories, can be either 'off-the-shelf' or custom-built. Both are different and address different levels of user demands. Applications such as ERP, CRM and BI, when implemented into any enterprise, are usually customized in order to make them gel with the business processes of that enterprise. It usually happens because of the scale and nature of a business.
- The experts often justify customization with 'one size does not fit all'. While off-the-shelf applications are primarily system software or in some cases application software which are deployed to execute basic tasks that do not need to gel into specific user environment. However, the classification and definition might differ. And there are broader dimensions to computer software that can further give insights into their function and role.
- To briefly understand, 'off-the-shelf' software packages, you can check out software packages such as 'Microsoft Office Suite' which include Word Processor, Spreadsheet and presentation tools that are ready to use and need no changes. But this is a small example. In bigger scenarios, 'off-the-shelf' software packages are the ones which are made to run in specific industries such as 'retail' where processes in every organization are similar.

1.4 Managing Hardware and Software Assets

Computer hardware and software must work together. Nothing useful can be done with the computer hardware on its own and computer software cannot be utilized without supporting hardware.

The following important points shows the relationships between computer hardware and software:
1. Both i.e. computer hardware and software are complementary to each other.
2. Except for upgrades hardware is normally a one-time expense, whereas software is a continuing expense.
3. Computer hardware and software are necessary for a computer to do useful job or task.
4. The same hardware can be loaded with different software to make a computer system perform different types of jobs or tasks.

Logical System Architecture

The logical architecture of a computer system is shown in Fig. 1.21. The architecture of computer system basically depicts the relationship among the hardware, system software, application software and users of computer system. As shown in Fig. 1.21, at the center of any computer system is the hardware, which comprises of the physical devices/components of the computer system.

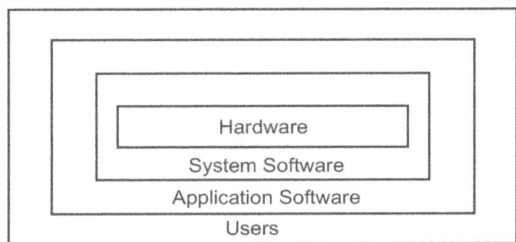

Fig. 1.21: Relationship between Computer Hardware,
System Software, Application Software and Users

Surrounding the hardware is the system software layer, which constitutes the operating and programming environment of the computer system. Surrounding the system software is the application software layer, which consists of a wide range of software, which are designed to do a specific task, or solve a specific problem. The final layer is the layer of users who normally interact with the computer system via the user interface provided by the application software.

1.4.1 Software

Software is instructions, (computer programs) that when executed provide desire function and performance. Software is a data structure that enables the programmer to adequately manipulate information. Software is documents that describe the operation and use of the programs.

1.4.1.1 Software Characteristics

Software is a logical rather than a physical system element. Therefore, software has characteristics that are considerably different than those of hardware. The main characteristics of software are:

1. Software is developed or engineered, it is not manufactured in the classical sense.
2. Software does not wear out.
3. Software is not susceptible to the environmental melodies.
4. Most software is custom-built, rather than being assembled from existing components.

1.4.1.2 Software Components

Computer software has information that exists in two basic forms:

1. Non machine-executable components and
2. Machine-executable components.

Software components are created through a series of translations that map customer requirements to machine-executable code. 'Reusability' is an important characteristics of a high-quality software component. That is, the component should be designed and implemented so that it can be reused in many different programs.

Software components are built using a programming language that has a limited vocabulary, an explicitly defined grammar and well-formed rules of syntax and semantics.

1.4.1.3 Types of Softwares

The instructions given to a computer is called **program**. The set of instructions, programs in a logical sequence is called **software**.

Classification of Softwares

System Software
1. Operating system
2. Utilities
3. Device drivers
4. Language translators

Application Software
1. Word Processor
2. Spreadsheet
3. Presentation graphics
4. Database Management
5. Integrated Package.

Computer software is a general term used to describe a collection of computer programs, procedures and documentation that perform some tasks on a computer system. The term includes application software such as word processors which perform productive tasks for users, system software such as operating systems, which interface with hardware to provide the necessary services for application software and middleware which controls and co-ordinates distributed systems.

"Software" is sometimes used in a broader context to mean anything which is not hardware but which is used with hardware, such as film, tapes and records.

Practical computer systems divide software systems into three majors classes: system software, programming software and application software, although the distinction is arbitrary and often blurred.

1. Application Software:

Application Software allows end users to accomplish one or more specific (non-computer related) tasks. Typical applications include industrial automation, business software, educational software, medical software, databases and computer games. Businesses are probably the biggest users of application software, but almost every field of human activity now uses some form application software.

Application software is a **set of one or more programs, used to solve a specific problem**. The program in an application software package are called **application programs** and the programmers who prepare application software are referred to as **application programmers.**

There are millions of application softwares available for a wide range of applications, ranging from simple applications, such as word processing, inventory management, preparation of tax returns, banking, hospital administration, insurance, publishing, to complex scientific and engineering applications.

Types of Application Software

Application software consist of following types:

1. **Personal Assistance Software:** A personal assistance software allows us to use personal computers for storing and retrieving our personal information and planning and managing our schedules, contacts, financial and inventory of important items.
2. **Graphics Software:** A graphics software enables user to use a computer system for creating, editing, viewing, storing, retrieving and printing designs, drawings, pictures, graphs and anything else that can be drawn in the traditional manner.
3. **Education Software:** Education software allows a computer system to be used as a teaching and learning tool.
4. **Word Processing Software:** A word-processing software enables user to make use of a computer system for creating, editing, viewing, formatting, storing, retrieving and printing documents.
5. **Database Software:** A database is a collection of related data stored and treated as a unit for information retrieval purposes. A database software is a set of one or more programs, which enable us to create a database, maintain it, organize its data in desired fashion and to selectively retrieve useful information from it.

6. **Spreadsheet Software:** A spreadsheet software is a numeric data analysis tool. It allows user to create a kind of computerized ledger.
7. **Entertainment Software:** Entertainment software allows a computer system to be used as an entertainment tool.

2. System Software:

System software helps to run the computer hardware and computer system. It includes operating systems, devices drivers, diagnostic tools, servers, windowing systems, utilities and more. The purpose of systems software is to insulate the applications program as much as possible from the details of the particular complex being used, especially memory and other hardware features and such as accessory devices as communications, printers, readers, displays, keyboards, etc.

System software is a **set of one or more programs, used to control the operation and extend the processing capability of a computer system**. System software performs one or more of the following functions:

1. Monitors the effective use of various hardware resources, such as CPU, memory, peripherals etc.
2. Supports the development of other application of software.
3. Supports the execution of other application software.

System software makes the operation of a computer system more effective and efficient. Programs in a system **software package** are called **system programs**, and the programmers who prepare system software are referred to a **system programmers.**

Types of System Software

System Software consist of following types:

1. **Communication software:** In a network environment, communications software enables transfer of data and programs from one computer system to another.
2. **Operating Systems:** Every computer system has an operating system software, which takes care of the effective and efficient utilization of all the hardware and software components of the computer system.
3. **Utility Programs:** Utility programs also known as **utilities**. Utility programs are a set of programs, which help users in system maintenance tasks, and in performing tasks of routine nature. Some of the tasks commonly performed by utility programs include formatting of hard disks or floppy disks, taking backup of files stored in hard disk on to a tape or floppy disk.
4. **Programming Language Translators:** Programming language translators are system software, which transform the instructions prepared by programmers in a programming language, into a form, which can be interpreted and executed by a computer system.

Comparison between Application Software and System Software:

Sr. No.	Application Software	System Software
1.	The program in an application software package are called application programs and the programmers who prepare application software are referred to as application programmers.	Programs in a system software package are called system programs, and the programmers who prepare system software are referred to a system programmers.
2.	Application software is a set of one or more programs, used to solve a specific problem.	Programs in a system software package are called system programs, and the programmers who prepare system software are referred to a system programmers.
3	Application Software allows end users to accomplish one or more specific (non-computer related) tasks.	System software helps to run the computer hardware and computer system. It includes operating systems, devices drivers, diagnostic tools, servers, windowing systems, utilities and more.
4.	Examples: (i) Word processing software (ii) Spreadsheet software	Examples: (i) Communication software (ii) Utility programs

1.4.2 Hardware

Fig. 1.22 shows different hardware parts of a computer system.

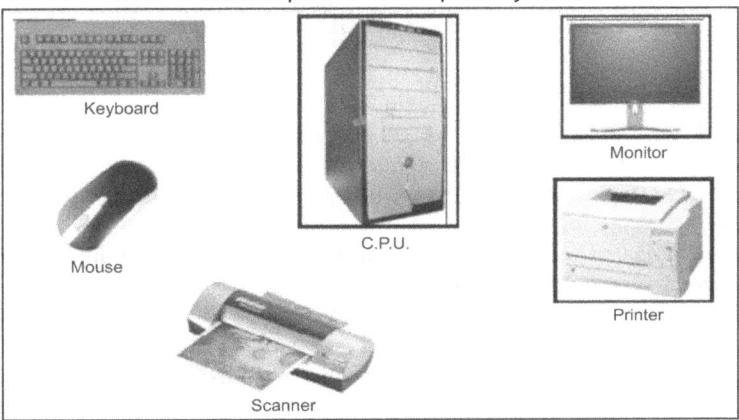

Fig. 1.22: Important Hardware Parts of a Computer System

The basic hardware parts of computers are as follows:

1. **Input Devices:**

The main functions of input devices are inputting the information to the computer in machine readable form. It is a device to enter information and instruction (a command or order given to the computer) i.e. data into computer from outside.

An input device performs the following functions:
(i) It accepts (i.e. reads) the list of instructions and data from the user.
(ii) It converts these instructions and data into binary form which is understood by the computer.
(iii) It supplies the converted instructions and data to the computer for further processing.

The input devices which are commonly used are:
(i) Punch Cards
(ii) Touchscreen
(iii) Mouse
(iv) Scanners
(v) Keyboard

1. Keyboard: The keyboard is the most commonly used input device today. Keyboards allow data entry into a computer system by pressing a set of keys which are neatly mounted on a keyboard, which is connected to the computer system. The most popular keyboard used today is the 101-keys as shown in Fig. 1.23.

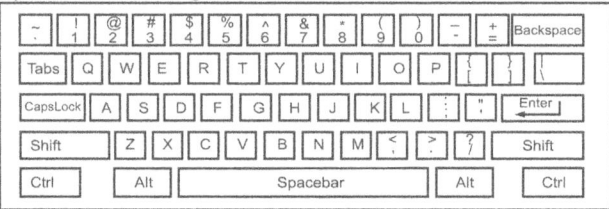

Fig. 1.23

A keyboard includes a standard set of printable characters i.e. standard keys and a number of non-text keys. Each of the standard keys functions itself, namely, each means something itself. On the other hand, the non-text keys are always used together with some of the standard keys.

2. Mouse: The name mouse, originated at the Stanford Research Institute, derives from the resemblance of early models to the common mouse. In computing, a mouse is a pointing device that functions by detecting two-dimensional motion relative to its supporting surface. Physically, a mouse consists of an object held under one of the user's hands, with one or more buttons. It sometimes features other elements, such as "wheels", which allow the user to perform various system-dependent operations or extra buttons or features can add more control or dimensional input.

The mouse's motion typically translates into the motion of a pointer on a display, which allows for fine control of a Graphical User Interface. Fig. 1.24 shows typical mouse.

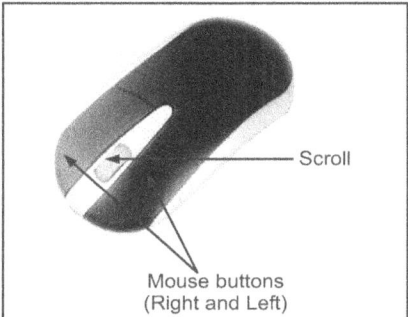

Fig. 1.24

3. Scanning Devices: This is most popular and important input device. The text, images or any data can be directly entered into computer memory with the help of scanners. There is no necessity of keying in the information, hence data entry is faster and more accurate. There are two types of scanners in use:

1. Optical scanners
2. Magnetic-ink character readers.

2. Central Processing Unit (CPU):

Central Processing Unit (CPU) is the heart of every computer system that performs the user instructions. There are three main sections:

(i) Primary storage section,
(ii) Arithmetic logic section,
(iii) Control unit.

(i) Primary Storage Section: This section is also called the main memory. It is used for four purposes and three are related to the data being processed.

(a) Data are fed into an input storage area where they are held until ready to be processed.
(b) A working storage space, that's like a sheet of scratch paper, is used to hold the data being processed and the intermediate results of such processing.
(c) An output storage area holds the finished results of the processing operations until they can be released.
(d) In addition to the above, the primary storage section also contains a program storage area that holds the processing instructions.

The programmer writing the application instructions determines how the space will be used for each job.

1. RAM (Random-Access Memory):

Random-access memory is a form of **computer data storage**. Today RAM takes the form of integrated circuits that allow the stored data to be accessed in any order. The word random thus refers to the fact that any piece of data can be returned in a constant time, regardless of its physical location and whether or not it is related to the previous piece of data.

RAM are of two types:
1. SRAM (Static RAM)
2. DRAM (Dynamic RAM)

2. ROM (Read Only Memory):

Read Only Memory is a class of storage media used in computers and other electronic devices. Because data stored in ROM cannot be modified, it is mainly used to distribute firmware.

(a) **PROM (Programmable Read-Only Memory):** A Programmable Read-Only Memory or Field Programmable Read-Only Memory (FPROM) is a form of digital memory where the setting of each bit is locked by a fuse or antifuse.

(b) **EPROM (Erasable Programmable Read-Only Memory):** An EPROM is a type of memory chip that retains its data when its power supply is switched-off. In other words, it is non-volatile. It is an array of floating-gate transistors individually programmed by an electronic device that supplies higher voltages than those normally used in digital circuits.

(c) **EEPROM:** EEPROM (also written as E^2PROM), which stands for Electrically Erasable Programmable Read-Only Memory, is a type of non-volatile memory used in computers and other electronic devices to store small amounts of data that must be saved when power is removed.

(ii) Arithmetic Logic Section: This section performs all calculations and decisions. Once data are fed into primary storage from input devices, they are held and transferred to the arithmetic-logic section where processing takes place. Intermediate results generated are placed in a designated working storage area until needed later on. Data may thus, move from primary storage to the arithmetic-logic unit many times, before the results are finalised. Once, finalised, the results are released to an output storage section and from there to an output device.

(iii) Control Section: By selecting, interpreting and seeing to the execution of program instructions, the control section, which acts as a central nervous system of the CPU, maintains order and directs the operation of the entire system; i.e. it knows when to feed data into the storage through the input device. The arithmetic-logic system knows what should be done with the data once it is received and finally results are obtained by the output devices.

3. Secondary Storage Devices:

To supplement the limited storage capacity of the primary storage section, most computers have secondary storage capabilities. These devices are connected directly to the processor which accept data/program instructions for the processor, retain them and then write them back to the processor as needed to complete the processing tasks.

4. Output Devices:

The result of computer processing is called as output. This result is communicated to the user through a device called an output device.

The following functions are performed by an output device:

(i) It accepts results produced by the computer which are in binary coded form and hence cannot be understood by us. For example, suppose we want to add the results of products A and B.

(ii) It converts these coded results to human readable form.

(iii) It supplies the converted form to the user.

The output devices which are commonly used are printer, plotter and VDU etc.

1. Printers: Although there are a number of ways printers can be classified, two common classifications are:

(i) The method used to place the image on the paper.

(ii) The speed of the printers. Both factors are important consideration in choosing a printer for a computer system.

Printers accomplish the task of placing on a page of paper in one of the two ways:

(i) Impact Printing.

(ii) Non-Impact Printing.

The selection of the printing method is directly related to the quality of print required, the speed necessary, and the cost factor.

    (a) Dot Matrix Printer: It is the most popular serial printer used with PCs. It has a print head that is pulled horizontally across the paper from left to right and back again by using a rubber belt and an electric motor. Dot matrix printer does not print a whole character but the character is generated from an array or matrix of dots which is usually 7 by 5.

    (b) Laser Printer: These are non-impact printers. They are widely used in application where high quality printing is required. The main aim of developing a laser printer was to eliminate the mechanical motion in the printer.

    (c) Ink Jet Printer: It is non-impact type of printer. It is similar to dot matrix printer. The image is produced by squirting ink through an array of tiny nozzles. In ink jet printers, the quality and resolution is directly dependent on the number of nozzles. The motive force for squirting the ink can either be an electromagnet or a piezo electric crystal. When a digital pulse of electricity is applied to the crystal it vibrates and causes the ink to squirt on the paper.

2. Monitors: A monitor contains a Cathode Ray Tube (CRT), hardware to control an electronics beam and a power supply. A CRT is used to display numbers, letters and graphics. CRT is consisting of an evacuated glass tube, conical in shape with a phosphor coating on the inside a large screen end and electron gun at the narrow end. The gun fires a narrow beam of electrons at the screen when the beam strikes the phosphor, light is emitted.

The LCDs (Liquid Crystal Displays) are compact, lightweight, durable and use little power. The disadvantage is that the LCD's graphics capability is poor because the individual pixels are not small enough to give sharp definition. LCD can have a maximum resolution equal to that of VGA resolution. They are very expensive.

The liquid crystal material is sandwiched between a pair of polarizers and transparent electrodes are deposited on either side of the sandwich. On one side the electrode lines are horizontal and on the other side the electrode lines are vertical. Applying a voltage between the horizontal electrode line and vertical electrode line creates an electric field across the liquid crystal just at the intersection where particular line of electrodes cross.

There are two types of LCD:
1. Passive-matrix LCD.
2. Active-matrix LCD.

1.4.2.1 Operating Systems

An operating system is an interface between hardware and user; an OS is responsible for the management and coordination of activities and the sharing of the resources of the computer. The operating system acts as a host for computing applications that are run on the machine. One of the purposes of an operation system is to handle the details of the operation of the hardware. This relieves application programs from having to manage these details and makes it easier to wire applications.

Operating systems offers a number of services to application programs and users. Applications access these services through Application Programming Interfaces (APIs) or System Calls. By invoking these interfaces, the application can request a service from the operating system, pass parameters and receive the results of the operation. Users may also interact with the operating system with some kind of software User Interface (UI) like typing commands by using Command Line Interface (CLI) or using a Graphical User Interface (GUI). For hand-held and desktop computers, the user interface is generally considered part of the operating system. On large multi-user systems like Unix and Unix-like systems, the user interface is generally implemented as an application program that runs outside the operating system.

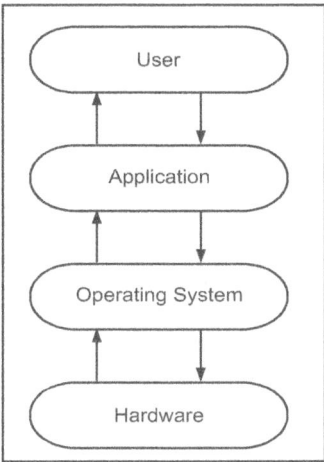

Fig. 1.25

1.4.2.2 Network Operating System

A Networking Operating System (NOS) is an operating system that contains components and programs that allow a computer running network operating system to serve requests from other computer for data, websites and provide access to other resources such as printer and file systems.

Features:
1. Add, remove and manage users who wishes to use resources on the network.
2. Allow users to access to the data on the network. This data commonly reside on the server.
3. Allow users to access data found on other network such as the internet.
4. Allow users to access to hardware connected to the network.
5. Protect data and services located on the network.

Network operating system features may include:
1. Basic support for hardware ports.
2. Security features such as authentication, authorization, login restrictions and access control.
3. Name services and directory services.
4. File, print, data storage, backup and replication services.
5. Remove access.

6. System management.
7. Network administration and auditing tools with graphic interfaces.
8. Clustering capabilities.
9. Fault tolerance and high availability.

1.4.2.3 Hardware Acquisition Process

Selection of a computer hardware and software requires the preparation of a specification for distribution to hardware and software vendors and a criteria for evaluating vendor proposals or specifications. The specification is presented to vendors in the form of an ITT (Invitation to Tender).

The ITT should include the following:

(i) Hardware requirements such as:
(a) CPU speed.
(b) Peripheral devices.
(c) Data preparation / input devices.
(d) Direct entry devices.
(e) Networking capability.

(ii) System software requirements, such as:
(a) Operating system software.
(b) Compilers.
(c) Program library packages.
(d) Database management packages.
(e) Communications software.
(f) Security/Access control software.

Types of Computers According to Hardware

- A computer is an electronic device which is used to store, retrieve and process data.
- Various uses of computers are:
    1. Computer are used in office automation.
    2. Computer are used in banking and business sectors.
    3. Computers used in advertising and entertainments.
    4. Computer are used in engineering, medical, science, sports and many more applications.

Types of computers are classified according to:

(i) Processing involved,

(ii) Technology implemented,

(iii) Size and processing speed.

Depending upon requirement, the processing involved in the machine can be of (i) Digital type, (ii) Analog type, (iii) Both digital and analog which is hybrid type. Hence, these calculating machines i.e. computers are of three types as given below.

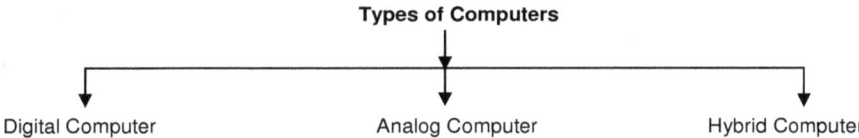

1. **Digital Computers:**

   In day-to-day life we use decimal number system to write numbers and do calculations. The digits in the numbers have fix place values like ten's place, hundred's place etc. Similarly in computer, binary number system is used to represent ON or OFF state of the electronic devices. The values in it have discrete nature and hence the calculations are exact and correct. In this counting processes are involved.

2. **Analog Computers:**

   The meaning of analogous is to show similarity. These computers show similarity between two observations or in comparisons. For example, the temperature is indicated by the expansion of mercury in the thermometer, speedometer shows the speed of a vehicle. The measurement of any quantity can not be absolute, it is always relative term. These computers do analogy with other data, hence are termed as analog computers, work on measurement.

3. **Hybrid Computers:**

   Analog processing machines are widely used to collect information. While the digital processing machines are superior from the point of mathematical calculations. In practice, combined analog and digital processing is used for special types of machines. These computers are called as hybrid computers. They are used in aeroplanes, submarines, hospitals, mines etc.

- **Classification of Computers**

    Computers can be classified mainly in four groups according to their shape and speed of processing.

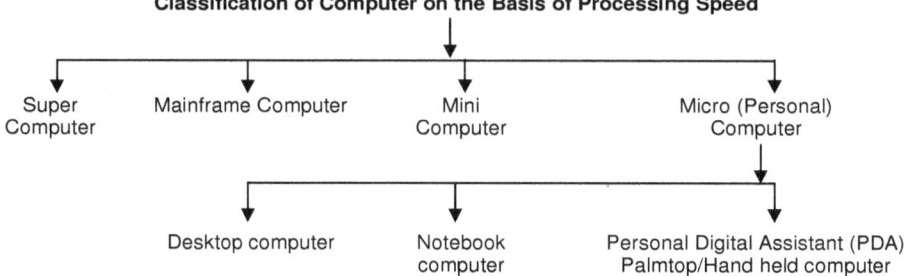

1. **Microcomputers:**

    Microcomputers are personal computers designed for an individual user. They are small in size. Personal computers are typically used for applications, such as word processing, spreadsheets, database management etc. With the addition of a modem and the use of telephone line, a personal computer becomes a terminal to the outside world, capable of retrieving information from internet.

    A personal computer is a non-portable, general purpose computer. It is generally designed to be used by one person at a time.

2. **Minicomputers:**

    Minicomputers are small to medium scale computers that is the midrange between a microcomputer and a mainframe. A mini-computer can support from a handful up to several hundred of user terminals. They are intrinsically designed as multi-user systems and are relatively easy to install and operate in multi-terminal environment. They are extensively used for pay-roll preparation, accounting and scientific computation.

3. **Mainframe Computer:**

    Mainframe computers are very powerful, large-scale general-purpose computers. Their word length may be 48,60 or 64 bits, memory capacity, 256 to 512 M byte, hard disk capacity 1 – 100 G byte or more and processing speed 100-200 MIPS. They are used where large amount of data are to be processed or very complex calculations are to be made and these tasks are beyond the capacities of mini computers. They are used in research organizations, large industries, airlines reservation where a large database has to be maintained.

    Mainframe computers are mainly used for handling the bulk of data and information processing of such organizations as insurance companies, banks, hospitals, railways etc.

4. Supercomputers:

Supercomputers processing capabilities lies in the large of 400-10,000 MIPS. Word length 64-96 bits, memory capacity 1024 M byte and more, hard disk capacity 1000 G byte and more. Supercomputers have limited use and limited market because of their very high price. They are being used at some research centers and government agencies involving sophisticated scientific and engineering tasks.

Super computers are the most powerful and expensive computers. They are primarily used for processing complex scientific applications. Supercomputers also support multiprogramming.

■■■

Chapter 2...

Managing Data Resources

Contents ...
2.1 Introduction
2.2 Organizing Data in a Traditional File Environment
2.3 The Database Approach to Management
2.4 Creating Database Environment
2.5 Database Trends

2.1 Introduction

- A group of symbol used to express a value of characteristic of an object is called data. A data which has been processed and organized so that it can be used to draw meaningful conclusion is called information.
- Example: 2225860 is a number data. When we say that it is a telephone number, then we get information from the data.
- Before we study managing data resources following terms must be known:
    1. **Bit:** A bit is Binary Digit (0, 1: Y,N: ON, OFF)
    2. **Byte:** A Byte is combination of BITS which represent a CHARACTER.
    3. **File:** File is collection of similar RECORDS.
    4. **Record:** Record is collection of FIELDS which reflect a TRANSACTION.
    5. **Database:** Database is an Organization's Electronic Library of FILES.

2.2.1 What is Data?

- Data is unstructured raw facts in isolation to be used as the raw material of the information system. Data is also the glue or mortar of the information system.
- Data could be expressed in numeric, alphabetic, alphanumeric, special characters, images, symbols or even voice. The various forms of data expressions are understood by the computer as strings of '0' or '1'. The computer works with electrical pulse OFF or ON, which state is equivalent to 'OFF' and 'ON' representing '0' and '1'. The '0' and '1' are known as Binary Digits or BITS. The computer uses strings made in combination of 'zeros' and 'ones' to move, store and compute the data.

| IT in Management | Managing Data Resources |

- The data is moved, stored and computed in the unit of bytes. One byte represents one character. The byte is made of eight bits. The data is structured for processing in a certain sequence and is ultimately stored in file.
    o The **Bits** from a **Byte**.
    o The **Byte** represents **Character**. A number of **Characters** forms a **Field**.
    o **Fields** constitute a **Record**.
    o **Records** constitute a **Block**.
    o **Blocks** constitute a **File**.
    o **Files** constitute a **Database**.

    Thus, the data hierarchy can be represented as follows:

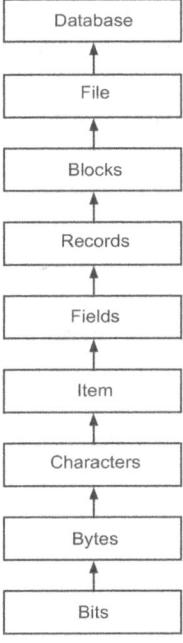

Fig. 2.1

2.2.2 Data Processing

- In data processing techniques sorting, relating, interpreting and computing items of data in order to provide meaningful and useful information. According to predefined procedures and rules data must be processed in specific order.

- The steps by which information data is expressed as data processed and returned to individuals as updated and useful information, is known as data processing. The following steps are mostly followed:
  1. Preparation of source documents.
  2. Input of data.
  3. Manipulation of data.
  4. Output of information.
  5. Storage.
  6. Maintenance.

  When you process data and get report you must apply the above steps.

1. **Preparation of source document:**

   First step is to obtain the data which are required for our system.

   For example: Employee code, name, address, phone number, age, sex, occupation etc. must be written down on the paper. These documents may be so designed that information is recorded in the required order.

2. **Input data:**

   Once the data has been extracted from source document, it is then fed to the computer so that processing can take place.

3. **Manipulation of data:**

   Whatever data fed to the computer may have to be classified or sorted. Instead of doing calculations, or pure computation, it is just a data manipulation.

   For example: Sort record according to designation. Departmentwise employee list etc. all these forms of data manipulation will produce results, which can be organized in the form of summaries.

4. **Output of information:**

   We print different reports which are helpful to the manager, accountant etc. Report must be understandable easily and quickly.

5. **Data storage:**

   Input data which are stored in computer must be used for preparation of different reports. Similarly, reports must be stored in one part of computer. It is useful for future use or reference. It is necessary for comparison of data before updating and after updating over different period of time. This means that data processing installations require a great deal of secondary storage space to store all the programs and different sets of data.

6. **Maintenance:**

   Whatever data stored in database must be maintained. Database does not contain garbage value, it cannot overflow etc. are the parts of database maintenance. Data is a vital importance to an organisation and may be confidential. Such confidential data must be accessed by unauthorized person for that data security must be important. For that different levels of security could be implemented for various types of data and operations. The enforcement of security could be datavalue dependent (e.g. a manager has access to the salary details of employees in his or her department only).

2.2.2.1 What is Data Processing?

- Data Processing involves a number of operations, similar to those in a manufacturing unit, to convert the basic raw material – data – into a finished product – Information. The typical data processing steps would include, among others, following activities.

Read	Sort	Collate	Compare	Store
Write	Merge	Delete	Decide	Display

Print	Copy	Enter	Compute	Etc.
Plot	Transfer	Create	Perform	

- Data processing also involves carrying out a number of data operations. To illustrate:

Operation	Brief Details
Capturing	Recording of data form an event/transaction.
Verifying	Checking/validating data for correctness.
Classifying	Placing data into specific categories.
Sorting/Arranging	Placing data in a particular sequence.
Summarising	Combining/aggregating data elements.
Calculating	Arithmetic/logical computations.
Storing	Placing data to some storage media.
Retrieving	Searching out and gaining access to specific data elements.
Reproducing	Duplicating data from one medium to another.
Disseminating/ Communicating	Transferring data from one place to another (device → user).

- Data Processing can be summarised as shown in Fig. 2.2.

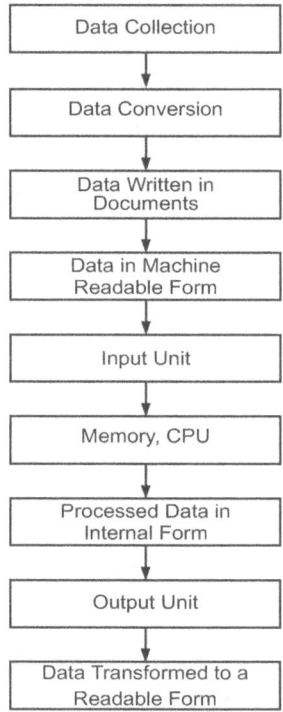

Fig. 2.2

2.2.2.2 Data Processing Hierarchy

- The data processing hierarchy consists of:
    1. Data Processing
    2. Office Automation System
    3. Transaction Processing System
    4. Management Information System
    5. Decision Support System
    6. Executive Support System Executive Information System
    7. Knowledge Based/Expert System
    8. Artificial Intelligence
    1. **Data Processing (EDP):** Data processing is the first sub-system in Business organisation aimed at processing transactions occurring due to day-to-day activities. Data processing is, however, now considered to be a lower level activity.

2. **Office Automation System (OAS):** It consists of activities/processes undertaken on computers for performing office routines.
3. **Transaction Processing System (TPS):** It is a computer-based system for capturing, classifying, storing, maintaining, updating and retrieving data for record keeping/inputs.
4. **Management Information System (MIS):** It is an organised set of processes for providing information for decision-makers and facilitating effective and efficient decision making.
5. **Decision Support System (DSS):** It is an interactive system providing information to managers to support operations and decision-making at strategic/tactical levels.
6. **Executive Informational Support System (EIS/ESS):** It combines data from both internal and external sources and communications environment that can be focussed and applied to a changing array of problems. Needless to add, EIS/ESS is meant for manager/ executives operating at Top levels.
7. **Knowledge Based/Expert Systems:** These systems rely on a knowledge base that is filled with rules of thumb or heuristic knowledge intuition, judgement and inferences about a specific area. These are interactive systems, aimed at helping problem resolution.

2.2.3 File Organisation

- File organisation used for files are:
    1. Serial
    2. Sequential
    3. Indexed Sequential
    4. Random (or Direct)

1. **Serial Organisation:**

   Serial files are stored in chronological order, that is as each record is received it is stored in the next available storage position. In general it is only used on a serial medium such as magnetic tape. This type of file organisation means that the records are in no particular order and therefore to retrieve a single record the whole file needs to be read from the beginning to end. Serial organisation is usually the method used for creating Transaction files (unsorted), Work and Dump files.

2. **Sequential Organisation:**

   Sequential files are serial files whose records are sorted and stored in an ascending or descending on a particular key field. The physical order of the records on the disk is not necessarily sequential, as most manufacturers support an organisation where certain records (inserted after the file has been set up) are held in a logical sequence but are physically placed into an overflow area. They are no longer physically contiguous with the preceding and following logical records, but they can be retrieved in sequence.

3. **Indexed Sequential Organisation:**

   Indexed Sequential file organisation is logically the same as sequential organisation, but an index is built indicating the block containing the record with a given value for the Key field. This method combines the advantages of a sequential file with the possibility of direct access using the Primary Key (the primary key is the field that is used to control the sequence of the records). These days manufacturers providing Indexed Sequential Software allow for the building of indexes using fields other than the primary key. These additional fields on which indexes are built are called Secondary Keys.

   There are three major types of indexes used:

   (i) **Basic Index:** This provides a location for each record (key) that exists in the system.

   (ii) **Implicit Index:** This type of index gives a location of all possible records (keys) whether they exist or not.

   (iii) **Limit Index:** This index groups the records (keys) and only provides the location of the highest key in the group. Generally they form a hierarchical index.

   Data records are blocked before being written to disk. An index may consist of the highest key in each block.

4. **Random or Direct:**

   A randomly organised file contains records arranged physically without regard to the sequence of the primary key. Records are loaded to disk by establishing a direct relationship between the key of the record and its address on the file, normally by use of a formula (or algorithm) that converts the primary key to a physical disk address. This relationship is also used for retrieval.

2.2.4 What is a Database?

- A database is a collection of related data elements such as, Tables (entities), Columns (fields or attributes), Rows (records). A database turns disparate pieces of data into information. Based on needs, Collect essential information, Principle of parsimony.
- Database is a collection of data. It contains information about one particular enterprise. Examples of enterprise and its database are:
  - Bank - Which stores bank data.
  - Hospital - Which stores patient data.
  - University - Which stores student data.

2.2.5 Database Management System

- A Database Management System (DBMS) is a computer program for managing a permanent, self-descriptive repository of data. This repository of data is called a database and is store in one or more files.
- Database Management System (DBMS) is collection of interrelated data and a set of programs to access the data.

- The objective of DBMS is to provide convenient and effective method of defining, storing and retrieving the information contained in the database. In addition the DBMS must provide for the safety of the information stored. It should protect the data from system crash or attempt at unauthorized access. If the data are to be shared among several users, the system must avoid possible anomalous results.

Examples of DBMS:
1. Oracle
2. Microsoft Access
3. SQL Server 2008.

- There are many reasons why you could use a DBMS:
    1. **Sharing between applications:** Multiple application programs can read and write data to the same database.
    2. **Crash recovery:** The database is protected from hardware crashes, disk media failures, and some user errors.
    3. **Security:** Data can be protected against unauthorized read and write access.
    4. **Sharing between users:** Multiple users can access the database at the same time.
    5. **Data distribution:** The database may be partitioned across various sites, organizations, and hardware platforms.
    6. **Extensibility:** Data may be added to the database without disrupting existing programs. Data can be reorganized for faster performance.
    7. **Integrity:** You can specify rules that data must satisfy. A D.B.M.S. can control the quality of its data over and above facilities that may be provided by application programs.

2.2.6 Structure of DBMS

- Components of DBMS are broadly classified as follows:
    1. **Query Processor:**
        (i) DML Pre-compiler
        (ii) Embedded DML Pre-compiler
        (iii) DDL Interpreter
        (iv) Query Evaluation Engine.
    2. **Storage Manager:**
        (i) Authorization and Integrity Manager
        (ii) Transaction Manager
        (iii) File Manager
        (iv) Buffer Manager.

3. **Data Structure:**
   (i) Data Files
   (ii) Data Dictionary
   (iii) Indices
   (iv) Statistical Data.

1. **Query Processor Components:**
   (i) **DML Pre-compiler:** It translates DML statements in a query language into low level instructions that query evaluation engine understands.

   It also attempts to transform user's request into an equivalent but more efficient form.

   (ii) **Embedded DML Pre-compiler:** It converts DML statements embedded in an application program to normal procedure calls in the host language.

   The Pre-compiler must interact with the DML compiler to generate the appropriate code.

   (iii) **DDL Interpreter:** It interprets the DDL statements and records them in a set of tables containing meta data or data dictionary.

   (iv) **Query Evaluation Engine:** It executes low-level instructions generated by the DML compiler.

2. **Storage Manager Components:**
- They provide the interface between the low-level data stored in the database and application programs and queries submitted to the system.

   (i) **Authorization and Integrity Manager:** It tests for the satisfaction of integrity constraints checks the authority of users to access data.

   (ii) **Transaction Manager:** It ensures that the database remains in a consistent state despite the system failures and that concurrent transaction execution proceeds without conflicting.

   (iii) **File Manager:** It manages the allocation of space on disk storage and the data structures used to represent information stored on disk.

   (iv) **Buffer Manager:** It is responsible for fetching data from disk storage into main memory and deciding what data to cache in memory.

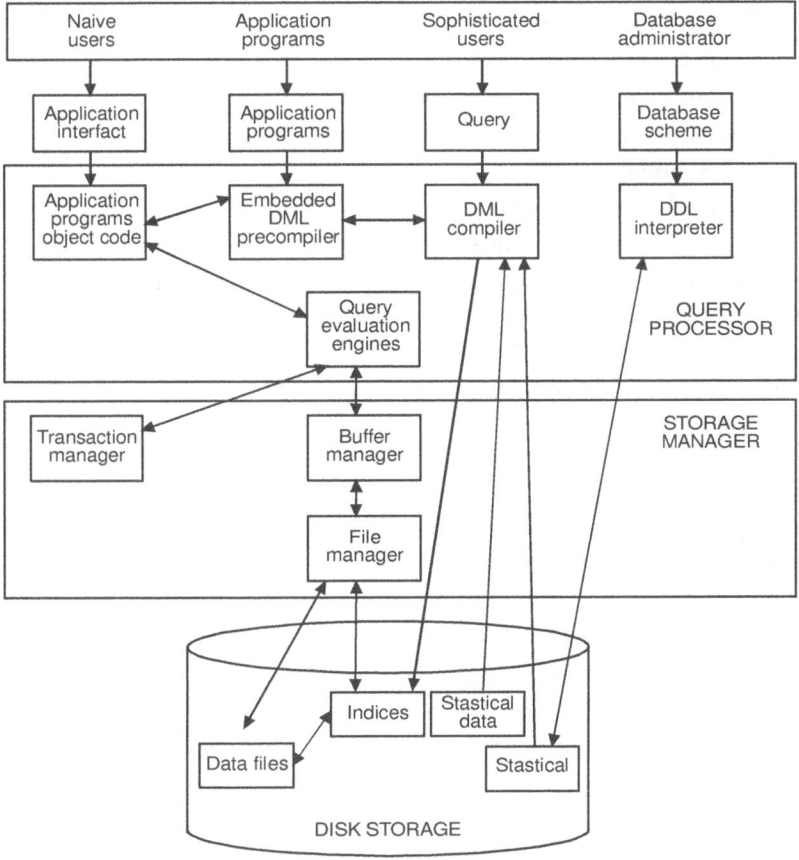

Fig. 2.3: DBMS Structure

3. **Data Structures:**

    Following data structures are required as a part of the physical system implementation.

    (i) **Data Files:** It stores the database.

    (ii) **Data Dictionary:** It stores meta data (data about data) about the structure of the database.

    (iii) **Indices:** Provide fast access to data items that hold particular values.

    (iv) **Statistical Data:** It stores statistical information about the data in the database. This information is used by query processor to select efficient ways to execute query.

2.2.7 Database Languages

Data sublanguage consists of two parts:
1. **Data Definition Language:** To specify the database schema.
2. **Data Manipulation Language:** To express database queries and updates.

1. **Data Definition Language:**

   Database schema is specified by a set of definitions which are expressed by a special language called Data Definition Language (DDL).

   (i) Data Dictionary: The result of compilation of DDL statements is a set of tables, which is stored in a special file called Data Dictionary or System Catalog. This file contain meta data i.e. data about data.

   (ii) Data Storage and Definition Language: The storage structure and access methods used by the database system are specified by a set of definitions in a special type of DDL called Data Storage and Definition Language.

2. **Data Manipulation Language:**

   DML is a language that enables users to access or manipulate data as organized by the appropriate data model.

   Data Manipulation means:
   - To retrieve the information from database.
   - To insert information into database.
   - To delete information from database.
   - To modify information from database.

   There are two types of DMLS:

   (i) Procedural DML: It requires a user to specify what data are needed and how to get those data.

   (ii) Non-procedural DML: It requires a user to specify what data are needed without specifying how to get those data.

   Query is a statement requiring or requesting the retrieval of information. Query language is the portion of DML that involves information retrieval.

2.2.8 SQL

- The SQL is used interactively to directly operate a database and produce the desired results. The user enters SQL command that is immediately executed. Most databases have a tool that allows interactive execution of the SQL language. These include SQL Base's SQL Talk, Oracle's SQL Plus and Microsoft's SQL server 7 Query Analyzer.

- The second way to execute a SQL command is by embedding it in another language such as Cobol, Pascal, BASIC, C, Visual Basic, Java etc. The result of embedded SQL command is passed to the variables in the host program, which in turn will deal with them. The combination of SQL with a fourth-generation language brings together the best of two worlds and allows creation of user interfaces and database access in one application.
- Regardless of whether, SQL is embedded or used interactively, it can be divided into three groups of commands, depending on their purpose.
    1. Data Definition Language (DDL).
    2. Data Manipulation Language (DML).
    3. Data Control Language (DCL).

1. **Data Definition Language:**
   Data Definition Language is a part of SQL that is responsible for the creation, updation and deletion of tables. It is responsible for creation of views and indexes also. The list of DDL commands is given below:

   CREATE TABLE
   ALTER TABLE
   DROP TABLE
   CREATE VIEW
   CREATE INDEX

2. **Data Manipulation Language:**
   Data manipulation commands manipulate (insert, delete, update and retrieve) data. The DML language includes commands that run queries and changes in data. It includes the following commands:

   SELECT
   UPDATE
   DELETE
   INSERT

3. **Data Control Language:**
   The commands that form data control language are related to the security of the database performing tasks of assigning privileges so users can access certain objects in the database.

   The DCL commands are:

   GRANT
   REVOKE
   COMMIT
   ROLLBACK

2.3 Creating Database Enviornment

- The Berkeley DB environment is created and described by the db_env_create() and DB_ENV->open()interfaces. In situations where customization is desired, such as storing log files on a separate disk drive or selection of a particular cache size, applications must describe the customization by either creating an environment configuration file in the environment home directory or by arguments passed to other DB_ENV handle methods.
- Once an environment has been created, database files specified using relative pathnames will be named relative to the home directory. Using pathnames relative to the home directory allows the entire environment to be easily moved, simplifying restoration and recovery of a database in a different directory or on a different system.
- Applications first obtain an environment handle using the db_env_create() method, then call theDB_ENV->open() method which creates or joins the database environment. There are a number of options you can set to customize DB_ENV->open() for your environment. These options fall into four broad categories:

Subsystem Initialization:

- These flags indicate which Berkeley DB subsystems will be initialized for the environment, and what operations will happen automatically when databases are accessed within the environment. The flags include DB_INIT_CDB, DB_INIT_LOCK, DB_INIT_LOG,DB_INIT_MPOOL and DB_INIT_TXN. The DB_INIT_CDB flag does initialization for Berkeley DB Concurrent Data Store applications. (See Concurrent Data Store introduction for more information.) The rest of the flags initialize a single subsystem; that is, when DB_INIT_LOCK is specified, applications reading and writing databases opened in this environment will be using locking to ensure that they do not overwrite each other's changes.

Recovery options:

- These flags, which include DB_RECOVER and DB_RECOVER_FATAL, indicate what recovery is to be performed on the environment before it is opened for normal use.

Naming options:

- These flags, which include DB_USE_ENVIRON and DB_USE_ENVIRON_ROOT, modify how file naming happens in the environment.

Miscellaneous:

- Finally, there are a number of miscellaneous flags, for example, DB_CREATE which causes underlying files to be created as necessary. See the DB_ENV->open() manual pages for further information.
- Most applications either specify only the DB_INIT_MPOOL flag or they specify all four subsystem initialization flags (DB_INIT_MPOOL, DB_INIT_LOCK, DB_INIT_LOG, and DB_INIT_TXN). The former configuration is for applications that simply want to use

the basic Access Method interfaces with a shared underlying buffer pool, but don't care about recoverability after application or system failure. The latter is for applications that need recoverability. There are situations in which other combinations of the initialization flags make sense, but they are rare.
- The DB_RECOVER flag is specified by applications that want to perform any necessary database recovery when they start running. That is, if there was a system or application failure the last time they ran, they want the databases to be made consistent before they start running again. It is not an error to specify this flag when no recovery needs to be done.
- The DB_RECOVER_FATAL flag is more special-purpose. It performs catastrophic database recovery, and normally requires that some initial arrangements be made; that is, archived log files be brought back into the filesystem. Applications should not normally specify this flag. Instead, under these rare conditions, the db_recover utility should be used.
- The following is a simple example of a function that opens a database environment for a transactional program.

```
DB_ENV *
db_setup(home, data_dir, errfp, progname)
    char *home, *data_dir, *progname;
    FILE *errfp;
{
    DB_ENV *dbenv;
    int ret;
    /*
     * Create an environment and initialize it for additional error
     * reporting.
     */
    if ((ret = db_env_create(&dbenv, 0)) != 0) {
        fprintf(errfp, "%s: %s\n", progname, db_strerror(ret));
        return (NULL);
    }
    dbenv->set_errfile(dbenv, errfp);
    dbenv->set_errpfx(dbenv, progname);
    /*
     * Specify the shared memory buffer pool cachesize: 5MB.
     * Databases are in a subdirectory of the environment home.
     */
```

```
        if((ret = dbenv->set_cachesize(dbenv, 0, 5 * 1024 * 1024, 0))!= 0)
        {
            dbenv->err(dbenv, ret, "set_cachesize");
            goto err;
        }
        if ((ret = dbenv->set_data_dir(dbenv, data_dir)) != 0) {
            dbenv->err(dbenv, ret, "set_data_dir: %s", data_dir);
            goto err;
        }
        /* Open the environment with full transactional support. */
        if ((ret = dbenv->open(dbenv, home, DB_CREATE |
         DB_INIT_LOG | DB_INIT_LOCK | DB_INIT_MPOOL | DB_INIT_TXN, 0))!= 0)
        {
            dbenv->err(dbenv, ret, "environment open: %s", home);
            goto err;
        }
        return (dbenv);
    err: (void)dbenv->close(dbenv, 0);
        return (NULL);
    }
```

2.4 Organizing Data in a Traditional File Environment

- An effective information system provides users with accurate, timely, and relevant information. Accurate information is free of errors. Information is timely when it is available to decision makers when it is needed. Information is relevant when it is useful and appropriate for the types of work and decisions that require it.
- Let's look at how information systems arrange data in computer files and traditional methods of file management.

2.4.1 File Organization Terms and Concepts

- A computer system organizes data in a hierarchy that starts with bits and bytes and progresses to fields, records, fries, and databases (see Fig. 2.4). A bit represent, the smallest unit of dam a computer can handle. A group of bits, called a byte, represents a single character, which can be a letter, a number, or another symbol. A grouping of characters into a Word, a group of words, or a complete number (such as a person's name or age) is called a field. A group of related fields, such as the students name, the course taken, the date, and the grade, makes up a record; a group of records of the same type is called a file.

- For example, the records in Fig. 2.4 could constitute a student course file. A group of related files makes up a database. The student course file illustrated in Fig. 2.4 could be grouped with fire, on students' personal histories and financial backgrounds to create a student database.
- A record describes an entity. An entity is a person, place, thing, or event about which we store and maintain information. Each characteristic or quality describing a particular entity is called an attribute. For example, Student_ID), Course, Date, and Grade are attributes of the entity COURSE. The specific values that these attributes can have are found in the fields of the record describing the entity COURSE.

> A computer system organizes data in a hierarchy that starts with the bit, which represents either a 0 or a 1. Bits can be grouped to form a byte to represent one character, number, or symbol. Bytes can be grouped to farm a field, and related fields can be grouped to form a record. Related records can be collected to form a file, and related files can be organized into a database.

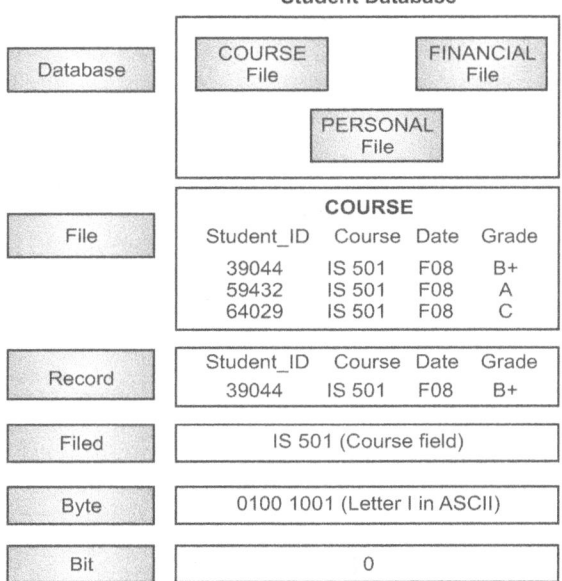

Fig. 2.4

2.4.2 Problems with the Traditional File Environment
- In most organizations, systems tended to grow independently without a company wide plan. Accounting finance, manufacturing, human resources, and sales and marketing all developed their own systems and data files. Fig. 2.5 illustrates the traditional approach to information processing.
- Each application, of' course, required its own files and its own computer programs to operate. For example, the human resources functional area might have a personnel

master file, a payroll tale, a medical insurance file, a pension file, a mailing list file, and so forth until tens, perhaps hundreds, of files arid programs existed. In the company as a whole, this process led to multiple master files created, maintained, and operated by separate divisions or departments. As this process goes on for five or ten years, the organization is saddled with hundreds of programs and applications that are very difficult to maintain and manage. The resulting problems are data redundancy and inconsistency, program-data dependence, inflexibility, poor data security, and an inability to share data among applications.

- **Data Redundancy and Inconsistency Data redundancy** is the presence of duplicate data in multiple data files so that the same data are stored in more than one place or location. Data redundancy occurs when different groups in an organization independently collect the same piece of data and store it independently of each other. Data redundancy wastes storage resources and also leads to data inconsistency, in which the same attribute may have different values. For example, in instances of the entity COURSE illustrated in Figure 6-1, the Date field might be updated in some systems but not in others. The same attribute, Student_ID, might also have different field names in different systems in the organization. Some systems might use Student ID and others might use ID, for example.

The use of a traditional approach to file processing encourages each functional area in a corporation to develop specialized applications. Each application requires a unique data file that is likely to be a subset of the master file or simply a file that is managed separately. These subsets of the master file lead to data redundancy and inconsistency, processing inflexibility, and wasted storage resources.

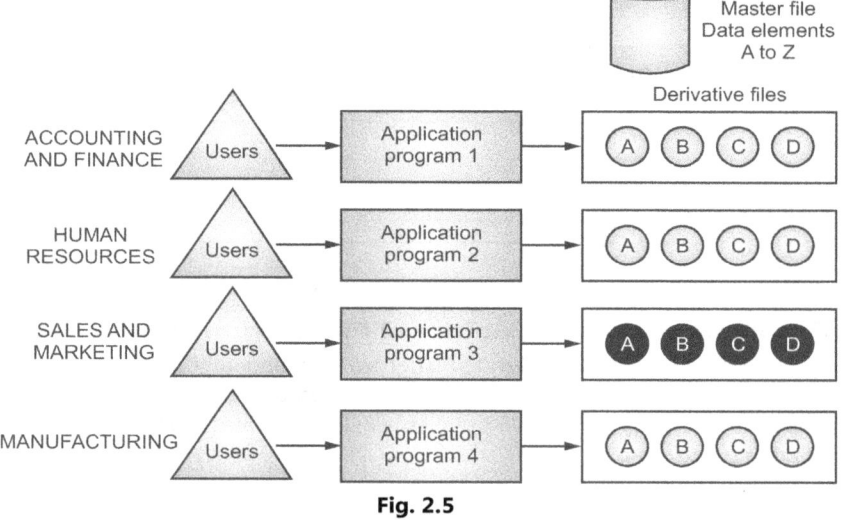

Fig. 2.5

- Additional confusion might result from using different coding systems to represent values for an attribute. For instance, the sales, inventory, and manufacturing systems of a clothing retailer might use different codes to represent clothing size. One system might represent clothing size as "extra large" while another might use the code "XL", for the same purpose. The resulting confusion would make it difficult for companies to create customer relationship management, supply chain management, or enterprise systems that integrate data from different sources.
- **Program-Data Dependence Program-data dependence** refers to the coupling of data stored in files and the specific programs required to update and maintain those files so that changes in programs require changes to the data. Every traditional computer program has to describe the location and nature of the data with which it works. In a traditional file environment, any change in it software program could require a change in the data accessed by that program. One program might be modified from a six-digit to a seven-digit postal code to incorporate the space between the first three and last three characters. If the original data file were changed from six-digit to seven-digit postal codes, other programs that required the six-digit postal code would no longer work properly. These changes would cost millions of dollars to implement properly.
- **Lack of Flexibility:** A traditional file system can deliver routine scheduled reports after extensive programming efforts, but it cannot deliver ad hoc reports or respond to unanticipated Information requirements in a timely fashion. The Information required by ad hoc requests is somewhere in the system but may be too expensive to retrieve. Several programmers might have to work for weeks to put together the required data items in a new life.
- **Poor Security:** Because there is little control or management of data, access to and dissemination of information may be out of control. Management may hare no way of knowing who is accessing or even making changes to the organization's data.
- **Lack of Data Sharing and Availability:** Because pieces of information in different files and different parts of the organization cannot be related to one another, it is virtually impossible for information to be shared or accessed in a timely manner. Information cannot flow freely across different functional areas or different parts of the organization. If users find different values of the same: piece of information in two different systems, they might not want' to use these systems because they cannot trust the accuracy of their data.

2.4.2 The Database Approach to Data Management

- Database technology cuts through many of the problems of traditional file organization. A more rigorous definition of a database is a collection of data organized to serve many applications efficiently by centralizing the data and managing redundant data. Rather than storing data in separate files for each application, data are stored so as to appear to users as being stored in only one location. A single database services multiple applications, For example, instead of a corporation storing employee data in separate information systems and separate files for personnel, payroll, and benefits, the corporation could create a single common human resources database.

2.4.2.1 Database Management Systems

- A Database Management Systems (DBMS) is software that permits an organization to centralize data, manage them efficiently, and provide access to the stored data by application programs. The DBMS acts as an interface between application programs and the physical data files. When the application program calls for a data item, such a, gross pay, the DBMS finds this item in the database and presents it to the application program. Using traditional data files, the programmer would have to specify the size and format of each data element used in the program and then tell the computer where they were located.
- The DBMS relieves the programmer or end user from the task of understanding where and how the data are actually stored by separating the logical and physical views of' the data, The logical view presents data as they would be perceived by end users OR business specialists while the physical view shows how data are actually organized and structured on physical storage media.
- The database management software makes the physical database available for different logical views required by users. For example, for the human resources database illustrated in Fig. 2.6, a benefits specialist might require a view consisting of the employee's name, social insurance number and supplemented health insurance coverage. A payroll department member might need data such as the employee's name, social insurance number, gross pay, and net pay. The data for all these views are stored in a single database where they call be more easily managed by the organization.

A single human resources database provides many different views of data, depending on the information requirements of the user. Illustrated are two possible views, one of interest to a benefits specialist and one of interest to a member of the company's payroll department.

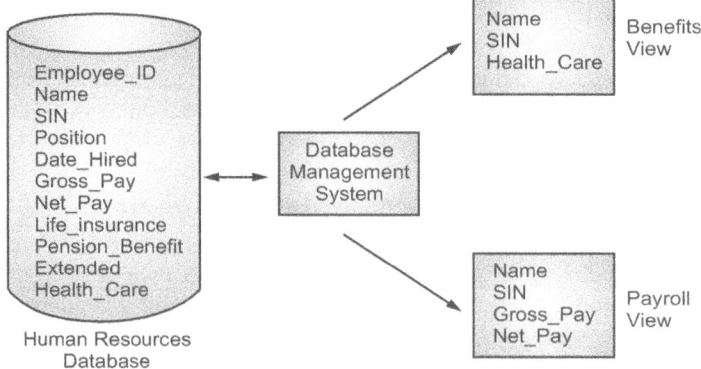

Fig. 2.6: Human resources database with multiple views

IT in Management   Managing Data Resources

- **How a DBMS Solves the Problems of the Traditional File Environment:** A DBMS reduces data redundancy and inconsistency by minimizing isolated files in which the same data are repeated. The DBMS may not enable the organization to eliminate data redundancy entirely, but it can help control redundancy by integrating various files into one DBMS. Even if the organization maintains some redundant data, using a DBMS eliminates data inconsistency because the DBMS can help the organization ensure that every occurrence of redundant data has the same values. The DBMS uncouples programs and data, enabling data to stand on their own. Access and availability of information will be increased and program development and maintenance costs reduced because users and programmers can perform ad hoc queries of data in the database. The DBMS enables the organization to centrally manage data, their use, and security through the use of a data dictionary (see below).

- **Relational DBMS:** Contemporary DBMS use different database models to keep track of entities, attributes, and relationships. The most popular type of DBMS today for PCs as well as for larger computers and mainframes is the relational DBMS. Relational databases represent data as two-dimensional tables (called relations). Tables are also referred to as files. Each table contains data on an entity and its attributes. Microsoft Access is a relational DBMS for desktop systems while DB2?, Oracle Database, and Microsoft SQL Server are relational DBMS for large mainframes and midrange computers. MySQL is a popular open-source DBMS and Oracle Database Lite is a DBMS for small handheld computing devices.

A relational database organizes data in the form of two-dimensional tables. Illustrated here are tables for the entities SUPPLIER and PART showing how they represent each entity and its attributes. Supplier Number is a primary key for the SUPPLIER table and a foreign key for the PART table.

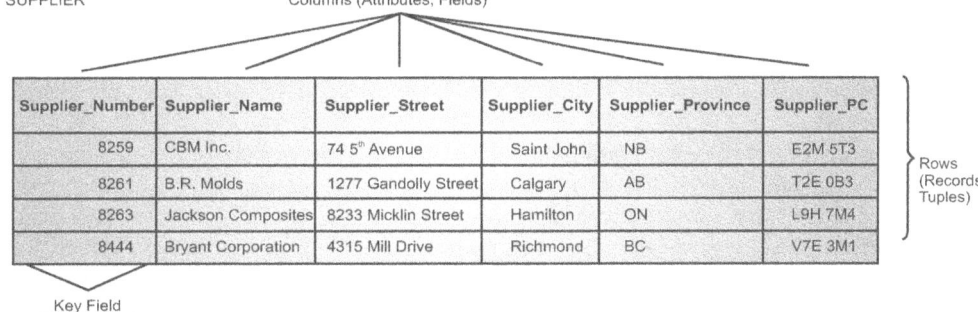

PART

Part Number	Part_Name	Unit_Price	Supplier_Name
137	Door latch	22.00	8259
145	Side mirror	12.00	8444
150	Door moulding	6.00	8263
152	Door lock	31.00	8259
155	Compressor	54.00	8261
178	Door handle	10.00	8259

Primary key   Foreign key

Fig. 2.7: Relational database tables

- Let us look at how a relational database organizes data about suppliers and parts (see Fig. 2.7). The database has a separate table for the entity SUPPLIER and a table for the entity PART. Each table consists of grid of columns and rows of data. Each individual element of data for each entity is stored as a separate field, and each field represents all attribute for that entity. Fields in a relational database are also called columns. For the entity SUPPLIER, the supplier identification number, name, street, city, province, and postal code are stored as separate fields within the SUPPLIER table, and each field represents an attribute for the entity SUPPLIER.
- The actual information about a single supplier that resides in a table is called a row. Rows are commonly referred to as records, or in very technical terms, as tuples. Data for the entity PART have their own separate table.
- The field for Supplier_Number in the SUPPLIER table uniquely identifies each record so that the record can be retrieved, updated, or sorted, and it is called a key field. Every table in a relational database has one field designated as its primary key. This key field is the unique identifier for all the information in any row of the table, and this primary key cannot be duplicated. Supplier_Number is the primary key for the SUPPLIER table, and Part_Number is the primary key for the PART table. Note that SUPPLIER_Number appears in both the SUPPLIER and PART tables. In the SUPPLIER table, Supplier_Number is the primary key. When the field Supplier-Number appears in the PART table, it is called foreign key and is essentially a lookup field to look Lip data about the supplier of a specific part.
- **Operations of a Relational DBMS:** Relational database tables can be combined easily to deliver data required by users, provided that any two tables share a common data element. Suppose we wanted to find in this database the names of suppliers who could provide us with part number 137 or part number 150. We would need information from two tables: the SUPPLIER table and the PART table. Note that these two files, have a shared data element: Supplier_Number.

- In a relational database, three basic operations, as shown in Fig. 2.8, are used to develop useful sets of data: select, join, and project. The select operation creates a subset consisting of all records in the file that meet stated criteria. Select creates, in other words, a subset of lows that meet certain criteria. In our example, we want to select records (rows) from the PART table where the Part_Number equals 137 or 150. The join operation combines relational tables to provide the user with more information than is available in individuals tables. In our example, we want to join the now-shortened PART table (only parts 137 or 150 will be presented) and the SUPPLIER table into a single new table.
- The project operation creates a subset consisting of columns in a table, permitting the user to create new tables that contain only the information required. In our example, we want to extract from the new table only the following columns: Part_Number, Part_Name, Supplier_Number and Supplier_Name.

The select, join and project operations enable, data from two different tables to be combined and only selected attributes to be displayed.

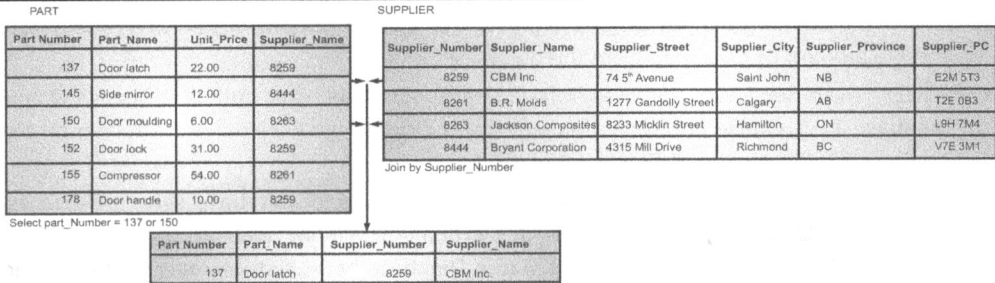

Fig. 2.8

- Object-Oriented DBMS Many applications today require databases that can store and retrieve not only structured numbers and characters, but also drawings, images, photographs, voice, and full-motion video. DBMS designed for organizing Structured data into rows and columns are not well suited to handling graphics-based or Multimedia applications. Object-oriented databases are better suited for this purpose.
- An object-oriented DBMS stores the data and procedures that act on those data as objects that can be automatically retrieved and shared. Object-oriented database management systems (OODBMS) are becoming popular because they can be used to manage the various multimedia components or lava applets used in Web applications, which typically integrate pieces of information from a variety of sources.
- Although object-oriented databases can store more complex types of information than relational DBMS, they are relatively slow compared with relational DBMS for processing large numbers of transactions. Hybrid object-relational DBMS systems are now available to provide capabilities of both object-oriented and relational DBMS.

- **Databases in the Cloud** Suppose your company wants to use cloud computing services. Is there a way to manage data in the cloud? The answer is a qualified "Yes." Cloud computing providers offer database management services, but these services typically have less functionality than their on-premises counterparts. At the moment, the primary customer base for cloud-based data management consists of Web-focused startups or small to medium sized businesses looking for database capabilities at a lower pi ice than a standard relational DBMS.
- Amazon Web Services has both a simple non-relational database called SimpleDB and a Relational Database Service, which is based on an online implementation of the MySQL open source DBMS. Amazon Relational Database Service (Amazon RDS) otters the full range of capabilities of MySQL. Pricing is based oil usage. (Charges run from 11 cents per hour for a small database using 1.7 GB of server memory to $3.10 per hour for a large database using 68 GB of server memory). There are also charges for the volume of data stored, the number of input-output requests, the amount of data written to the database, and tile amount of data read from the database.
- Amazon Web Services additionally offers Oracle customers the option to license Oracle Database 11 g, Oracle Enterprise Manager, and Oracle Fusion Middleware to run oil the Amazon EC2 (Elastic Cloud Compute) platform.
- Microsoft SOL Azure Database is a cloud-based relational database service based oil Microsoft's SOL Server DBMS. It provides a highly available, scalable database service hosted by Microsoft in the cloud. SQL Azure Database helps reduce costs by integrating with existing software tools and providing symmetry with on-premises and cloud databases.
- TicketDirect which sells tickets to concerts, sporting events, theatre performances, and movies in Australia and New Zealand, adopted the SQL Azure Database cloud platform in order to improve management of peak system loads during major ticket sales. It migrated its data to the SQL Azure database. By moving to a Cloud Solution, TicketDirect is able to scale its computing resources in response to real-time demand while keeping costs low.
- Ofcourse, there is a downside to using databases located in the cloud. When the cloud is down or unavailable, businesses cannot access their data. Recently, Amazon's cloud was down for a period that ranged front 11 hours to five days for then, customers that used some of their Eastern-U.S.-based Elastic Cloud Computer (EC2) services. What would your company do if its cloud-based databases were unavailable? What sort of backup data would you need? Where would it be stored, and how would it be accessed? These are just some of the questions to be answered before putting critical databases on the cloud.

2.4.2.2 Capabilities of Database Management Systems

- A DBMS includes tools for organizing, managing, and accessing the data in the database. The most important are its data definition language, data dictionary, and data manipulation language.

> Microsoft Access has a rudimentary data dictionary capability that displays information about the size, format, and other characteristics of each field in a database. Displayed here is the information maintained in the SUPPLIER table. The small key icon to the left of supplier – Number indicates that its a key field.

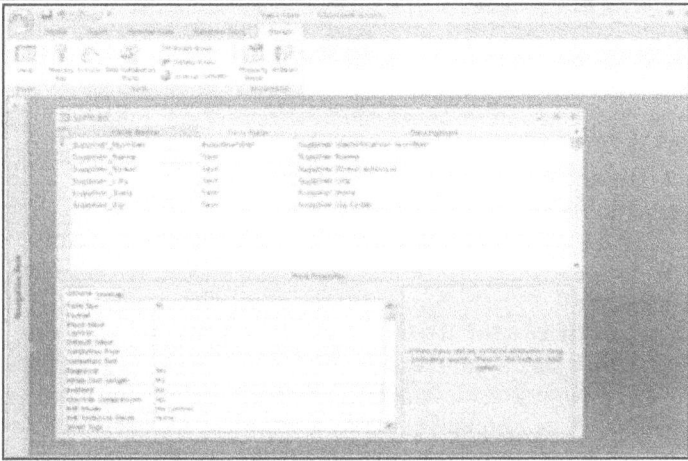

Fig. 2.9

- DBMS have a data definition capability to specify the structure of the content of the database. It would be used to create database tables and to define the characteristics of the fields in each table. This information about the database would be documented in a data dictionary, an automated or manual file that stores definitions of data elements and their characteristics.

- Microsoft Access has a rudimentary data dictionary capability that displays information about the name, size, type, format and other properties of each field in a table (see Fig. 2.9). Data dictionaries for large corporate databases may capture additional Information, such as usage; ownership (who in the organization is responsible for maintaining the data); authorization; security; and the individuals, business functions, Programs, and reports that use each data element.

- Querying and Reporting DBMS include tools for accessing and manipulating information in databases. Most DBMS have a specialized language called a data manipulation language that is used to add, change, delete, and retrieve the data in the database.

- This language contains commands that permit end users and programming specialists to extract data from the database to satisfy information requests and develop applications. The most prominent data manipulation language today is Structured Query Language, or SQL. Fig. 2.10 illustrates the SQL query that would produce the new table in Fig. 2.7. You call find out more about how to perform SQL queries in our Learning Tracks for this chapter.
- Users of DBMS for large and midrange computers, such as D32, Oracle, or SQL Server, would use SQL to retrieve information they need from a database. Microsoft Access also uses SQL but it provides its own set of user-friendly tools, for querying databases (known as Query by Example or QBE) and for organizing data from databases into more polished reports.

Designing Databases
- To create a database, you must understand the relationships among ; the data, the type of data that will be maintained in tile database, how the data will be Used, and how the organization will need to change to manage data from a company-wide perspective. The database requires both a conceptual design arid a physical design. The conceptual, or logical, design of a database is an abstract model of the database from a business perspective; the physical design shows how the database is actually arranged on direct - access storage devices.

2.4.2.3 Normalization and Entity-Relationship Diagrams

- The conceptual database design describes how the data elements in the database are to be grouped. The design process identifies relationships among data elements and the most efficient way of grouping data elements to meet business information requirements. The process also identifies redundant data elements and the groupings of data elements required for specific application programs. Groups of data are organized, refined, and streamlined until an overall logical view of the relationships among all the data in the database emerges.
- To use a relational database model effectively, complex groupings of data must be streamlined to minimize redundant data elements and awkward many-to-many relationships. The process of creating small, stable, yet flexible and adaptive data structures from complex groups of data is called normalization. Fig. 2.10 and 2.11 illustrate this process.

A unnormalized relation contains repeating groups. For example, there can be many parts and suppliers for each order. There is only a one-to-one correspondence between Order_Number and Order_Date.

ORDER (Before Normalization)

Order_Number	Order_Date	Part_Number	Part_Name	Unit_Price	Part_Quantity	Supplier_Number	Supplier_Name	Supplier_Street	Supplier_City	Supplier_Province	Supplier_PC

Fig. 2.10

- In the particular business modelled here, all order can have more than one part, hut each part is provided by only one supplier. If we band a relation called ORDER with all the

IT in Management

Managing Data Resources

fields included here, we would have to repeat the name and address of the supplier for every part oil the order, even though the order is for parts from a singles upplier. This relationship contains repeating data groups, so called because there call be many parts on a single order to a given supplier. A mare efficient way to arrange the data is to breakdown ORDER into smaller relations, each of which describes a single entity. If we got step by step and normalize the relation ORDER, we emerge with the relations illustrated in Fig. 2.10. You can find out more about normalization, entity-relationship diagramming, and database design in the Learning Tracks for' this chapter.

- Relational database systems try to enforce referential integrity rules to ensure that relationships between coupled tables remain consistent. When one table has a foreign key that points to another table, you may not add a record to the table with the key unless there is a Corresponding record in the linked table. In the database we examined earlier in this chapter, the foreign key Supplier_Number links the PART table to the SUPPLIER table. We may not add a new record to the PART table for part with Supplier_Number 8266 unless there is a corresponding record in the SUPPLIER table for Supplier_Number 8266. We must also delete the corresponding record in the PART table it we delete the record in the SUPPLIER table for Supplier_Number 8266. In other words, we should not have parts from non-existent suppliers!

- Database designers document their data model with all entity-relationship diagram, illustrated in Fig. 2.11. This diagram illustrates the relationships among the entities SUPPLIER, PART, LINE_ITEM and ORDER. The boxes represent entities. The lines connecting the boxes represent, relationships. A line connecting two entities that ends in two short marks designates a one-to-one relationship. A line connecting two entities that ends with a crow's foot topped by a short mark indicates a one-to-many relationship. Fig. 2.12 shows that one ORDER can contain many LINL_ITEMS. (A PART can be ordered many times and appear many times as a line item in a single order). Each PART can have only one SUPPLIER, but many PARTs can he provided by the same SUPPLIER.

After normalization, the original relation ORDER has been broken down into four smaller relations. The relation ORDER is left with only two attributes and the relation LINE_ITEM has a combined, or concatenated, key consisting of Order Number and Part-Number.

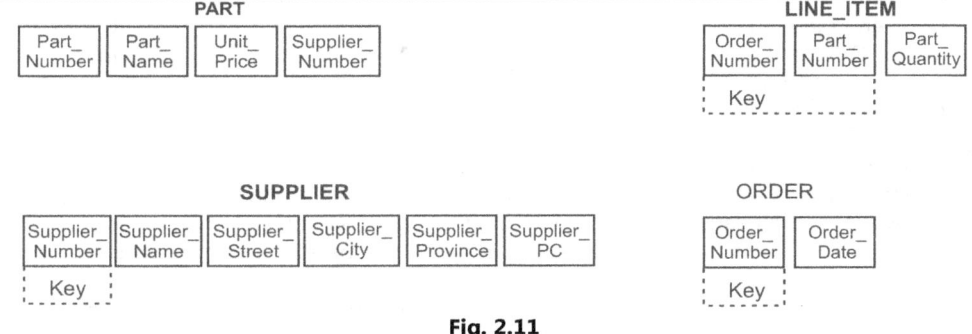

Fig. 2.11

> This diagram shows the relationships among the entities SUPPLIER, PART, LINE_ITEM and ORDER that might be used to model the database in Fig. 2.12.

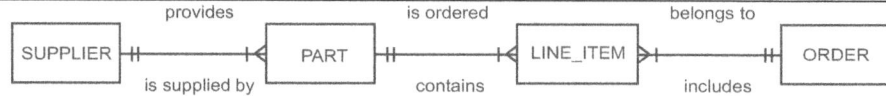

Fig. 2.12

- It cannot he emphasized enough if the business does not get its data model right, the system will not be able to serve the business well. The Company's system, will not be as effective as they could be because they will have to work with data that may be inaccurate, incomplete, or difficult to retrieve. Understanding the organization's data and how they should be represented in a database is perhaps the most important lesson you can learn from this course.

2.5 Current and Future Database Trends

- In the late 1960s and early 1970s, there were two mainstream approaches to constructing Database Management System's (DBMS's). The first approach was based on the hierarchical data model, typified by IMS (Information Management Systems) from IBM, in response to the enormous information storage requirements generated by the Apollo space program. The second approach was based on the network data model, which attempted to create a database standard and resolve some of the difficulties of the hierarchical model, such as its inability to represent complex relationships DBMSs. However, these two models had some fundamental disadvantages:
    - Complex programs had to be written to answer even simple queries
    - There was minimal data independence
    - There was no widely accepted theoretical foundation.
- Many experimental relational DBMS were implemented thereafter, with the first commercial products appearing in the 1970's and early 1980's. Relational DBMSs are referred to as second-generation DBMSs. Relational DBMS technology used extensively in the 80's and 90's was limited in meeting the more complex entity and data needs of companies, as their operations and applications became increasingly complex. In response to the increasing complexity of database applications, two "new" data models have emerged; the Object-Relational Database Management Systems (ORDBMS) and Object-Oriented Database Management Systems (OODBMS), which subscribes to the relational and object data models respectively. The OODBMS and ORDBMS have been combined to represent the third generation of Database Management Systems.
- There is considerable debate between OODBMS and RDBMS proponents as to the adequacies of these applications. The OODBMs proponents claim that RDBMs are satisfactory for standard business applications but lack the capability to support complex applications. The relational supporters claim that relational technology is a necessary part of any real DBMS and that complex applications can be handled by extensions to the relational model.
- Recent database trends include the growth of distributed databases and the emergence of object-oriented and hyper-media databases.

2.5.1 Distributed databases

- The growth of distributed processing and networking has been accompanied by a movement towards distributed database. A distributed database is one, which is stored in more than one physical location. Parts of the database are stored physically in one location, and other parts are stored and maintained in other locations. There are two main ways of distributing a database. The central database can be partitioned so that each remote processor has the necessary data to serve its local area. Changes in local files can be justified with the central database on a batch basis, often at night.
- Another strategy is to replicate the central database at all remote locations. This strategy also requires updating of the central database off hours.
- Both distributed processing and distributed databases have benefits and drawbacks. Distributed systems reduce the vulnerability of a single, massive central site. They permit increases in systems' power by purchasing smaller less expensive computers.
- Finally, they increase service and responsiveness to local users. Distributed systems, however, are dependent on high quality telecommunication lines, which themselves are vulnerable. Moreover, local databases can sometimes depart from central data standards and definitions, and they pose security problems by widely distributing access to sensitive data. The economies of distribution can be lost when remote sites buy more computing power than they need. Despite these drawbacks, distributed processing is growing rapidly.

2.5.2 Object Oriented and Hybrid Models

- These models have emerged in an attempt to store, search and manipulate data about objects, which have complex inner data structures. Object-oriented database management systems (OODBMS) are systems which are designed from scratch, whereas hybrid DBMS are some combination of RDBMS and OODBMS.
- Traditional DBMS including RDBMS store just data, without the procedures required to manipulate the data. This provided the long sought-after in-dependence between application programs and their operational data. In contrast, OODBMS store objects. An object contains data about an entity, and also the methods that process those data. An object may be anything to which a concept applies, e.g. a number, a document, a vector, a sound or an image.
- Whereas in conventional DBMS, any kind of procedure can access the data (a consequence of data independence), in OODBMS the data can only be accessed through the methods stored with them as part of a class. Objects can be composed of other objects, which in turn can be composed of other objects, and so on. This enables the capture of highly complex data structures.
- A major difference between the two approaches is that RDBMS databases are passive, meaning that they contain only data. OODBMS databases, on the other hand, are active, because an attempt to read or update the data would trigger certain actions automatically.

- Unlike the relational data model, the object-oriented data model is not based on a formal mathematical model, but is a collection of concepts such as data and behaviour encapsulation, inheritance, reuse and message passing, which have proved to be of great use in developing applications. These and other concepts allow the OODBMS to capture more of the semantics of the real world.
- However, although OODBMS have significant strengths, they are not free of limitations, the foremost of which is the lack of a strong underlying theory. Further, for OODBMS there still exists the lack of a standardized easy-to-use query language.
- Object oriented and hypermedia databases can store graphics and other types of data in addition to conventional text data to support multimedia applications. Hyper media databases allow data to be stored in nodes linked together in any pattern established by the user. Web sites use a hypermedia database approach to store information as interconnected pages containing text, sound, video and graphics.
- In the future databases will be required to store and retrieve not only structured numbers and characters but also drawings, images, photographs, voice, and full motion video e.g., object oriented multi-media database.

2.5.3 Multi-dimensional Data Analysis

- Multi-dimensional databases are a compact and easy-to-understand way of visualizing and manipulating data elements that have been inter-relationships. Multi-dimensional structures are best visualized as cubes of data, and cubes within cubes of data. Each side of a cube is a dimension.

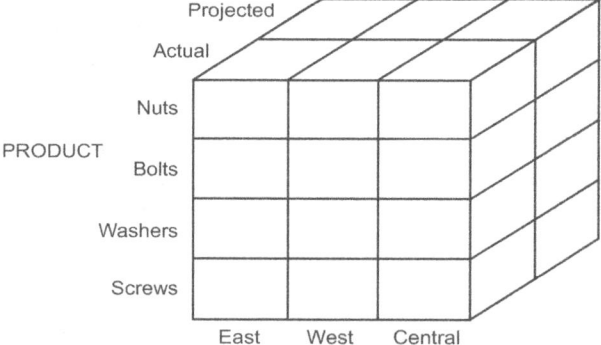

Fig. 2.13

- The cube can be expanded to include other dimensions, for example a company selling four different products, in four different regions, might want to know actual sales by product for each region and might also want to compare them with projected sales. This analysis requires a multi-dimensional view of data. Each aspect of information/product, pricing, cost, region, or time period – represents a different dimension so a product manager could use a multi-dimensional data analysis tool to learn how much of a product was sold in a certain region, in a certain month, how that compares with the previous month and the same month of last year, and how it compares with the sales forecast.

2.5.4 Data Warehouse

- A data warehouse is a database, with tools, that stores current and historical data of potential interest to managers throughout the company. The data originates in many core operational systems and external sources and are copied into the data warehouse databases as often as needed.
- The data is standardized and consolidated so that it can be used across the enterprise for management analysis and decision-making. The data is available for anyone to access as needed but cannot be altered. A data warehouse system includes a range of ad hoc and standardized query tools, analytical tools, and graphical reporting facilities. These systems can perform high-level analysis of patterns or trends, but they can also drill into more details when needed. Database warehouses not only offer improved information, but also they make it easy for decision makers to obtain it. They even include the ability to model and remodel the data. These systems also enable decision makers to access data as often as they need without affecting the performance of the underlying operational systems.

2.5.5 Linking Databases to the Web

- It has been estimated that 70 percent of the world's business information resides on mainstream databases, many of which are older legacy systems. Many of these legacy systems use hierarchical DBMS or even traditional flat files where information is difficult for users to access. A new series of software products has been developed to help users gain access to this mountain of legacy data through the Web.
- There are a number of advantages to using the Web to access an organisation's internal database. Web browser software is extremely easy to use, requiring much less training than even user-friendly database query tools. The web interface requires no changes to the legacy database. Companies leverage their investments in older systems because it cost much less to add a Web interface in front of a legacy system than to redesign and rebuild the system to improve user access.

■■■

Chapter 3...

Networking

Contents ...

3.1 Introduction
    3.1.1 Definition
    3.1.2 Components of Network
    3.1.3 Advantages
    3.1.4 Disadvantages
3.2 Importance of Networking
3.3 Computer Networks / Types of Computer Networks
    3.3.1 Local Area Network (LAN)
    3.3.2 Wide Area Network (WAN)
    3.3.3 Metropolitan Area Network (MAN)
3.5 Network Topology
    3.5.1 Bus Topology
    3.5.2 Star Topology
    3.5.3 Ring Topology
    3.5.4 Mesh Topology
    3.5.5 Tree Topology
    3.5.6 Hybrid Topology
3.6 Wireless Networks
    3.6.1 Types of Wireless Networks

3.1 Introduction

- A computer network, or simply a network, is a collection of computers and other hardware interconnected by communication channels that allow sharing of resources and information.
- When one process in one device is able to send/receive data to/from one process residing in a remote device, the two devices are said to be networked.
- A network is a group of devices connected to each other. Networks may be classified into a wide variety of characteristics like the medium used to transport the data, communications protocol used, scale, topology, benefit, and organizational scope.

- Communication protocols define the rules and data formats for exchanging information in a computer network, providing the basis for network programming.
- Network means a collection of interconnected computer network of stand-alone computers.
- A computer network is interconnection of various computer systems located at different places. In computer network two or more computers are linked together with a medium and data communication devices for the purpose of communication of data and sharing resources.

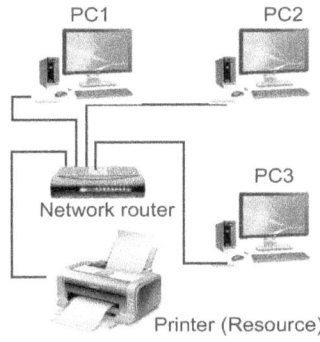   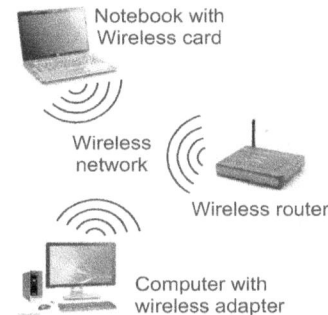

(a) **Typical wired network**   (b) **Wireless network**

Fig. 3.1

3.1.1 Definition

- "A group of computers connected in same fashion in order to share resources is called as computer network".

OR

- "A collection of autonomous computers interconnected by a single technology" is known as computer network. Two computers are said to be interconnected if they are able to exchange information.

OR

- **Network is a group of computers and associated peripheral devices connected by a communications channel capable of sharing files and other resources among several users.**

3.1.2 Components of Network

- A computer network is exchange of data between two computer machines. A computer network is made up of five components. This is shown in Fig. 3.2.
    1. **Sender:** This is the device which sends the data message. It can be a computer, workstation, telephone handset, video camera and so on. Data is in human readable form, gets converted into machine form i.e. 0's and 1's.

2. **Receiver:** The receiver is the device which receives the message. Again it can be a computer, workstation, telephone handset, television and so on.

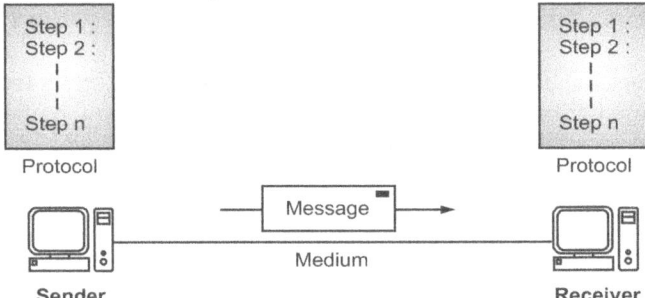

Fig. 3.2: Components of computer network

3. **Message:** The message is nothing but the data or information which is to be communicated. It may have texts, numbers, pictures, sound or video or combination of anything from these.
4. **Medium:** The transmission medium is the physical path by which a message travels from sender to receiver. It may be twisted pair wire, coaxial cable, fiber-optic cable, laser or radio waves and so on. The radio waves may be terrestrial or satellite microwave.
5. **Protocol:** A protocol is a set of rules required for data communication. It represents the agreement between the two communicating devices. Without protocol, we can connect two devices but they cannot communicate with each other. For example, without a translator, a Japanese cannot communicate with a French person. The job of protocol is similar to the translator.

3.1.3 Advantages

1. Networking provides the advantage of centralization of data from all the user systems to one system where it can be managed in an easy and better way.
2. Using networking peripherals such as printers can be shared amongst many different users.
3. Communication across the network is cheap and fast.
3. Networking terminals are cheaper than standalone PCs.
5. Using networking software can be shared amongst different users.
6. Networking provides a flexible networking environment. Employees can work at home by using through networks ties through networks into the computer at office.
7. Networking also provides the function of back-up.
8. Networking supports increased storage capacity since there is one or more computers which can easily share files.

3.1.4 Disadvantages

1. Proper maintenance of a network requires considerable time and expertise.
2. Security threats are always problems with large networks. There are hackers who are trying to steal valuable data of large companies for their own benefit.
3. One major disadvantage of networking is the breakdown of the whole network due to an issue to the server, therefore once established the network it is vital to maintain server properly to prevent such disastrous breakdowns.
4. Security measures are needed to restrict access to the network.
5. Computer networks are expensive to set up.
6. Since, most networks have client/server architecture, the client users lack any freedom, as centralized decision making sometimes hinder how a client wants to use his computer.
7. Networks need efficient handlers i.e. any user with just the basic skills cannot operate/administer a computer network.

3.2 Importance of Networking

- In today's competitive market, responsiveness to customer or supplier demand is often a decisive factor in the success of an organization.
- The network is considered one of the most critical resources in an organization, both in the private and public sectors.
- Networks are created to provide a means to satisfy an objective or goal or need. These objectives and needs are frequently critical, therefore the network itself is critical. Consider the metaphor of a transportation network (roads, highways, rails, and so on). If any of these conduits were to become suddenly unavailable, our ability to distribute food, clothes and products would be seriously compromised. The residents of a town or country who need the food, clothes and products are the end users of this particular type of network.
- Similarly, a computer network is created to provide a means of transmitting data, sometimes essential data, from one computer to another. The accuracy and speed of daily business transactions for large organizations are vital to their success. Unscheduled disruption resulting in the failure to process these daily business transactions are costly and potentially disastrous.
- The widespread use of networks extends the reach of organizations. These remote interactions with customers, suppliers and business partners have significantly benefited countless businesses. It has correspondingly positively impacted the overall productivity of many countries. Such productivity gains, however, are only as good as the network.

Need of Computer Networks?

- Computer networks help users on the network to share the resources and in communication. Can you imagine a world now without emails, online news papers, blogs, chat and the other services offered by the internet?
- The following are the important reasons that describe the need of computer network in today's world:
    1. **File sharing:** Networking of computers helps the users to share data files.
    2. **Hardware sharing:** Users can share devices such as printers, scanners, CD-ROM drives, hard drives etc.
    3. **Application sharing:** Applications can be shared over the network, and this allows to implement client/server applications
    4. **User communication:** Networks allow users to communicate using e-mail, newsgroups, and video conferencing etc.
    5. **Network gaming:** Lot of games are available, which supports multi-users.

3.3 Computer Networks / Types of Computer Networks

- Fig. 3.3 shows categories of computer networks.

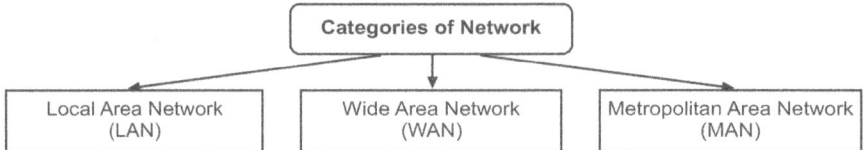

Fig. 3.3: Types of networks

3.3.1 Local Area Network (LAN)

- LAN is a group of computers and associated peripheral devices connected by a communications channel, capable of sharing files and other resources among several users.
- A Local Area Network (LAN) is a computer network that interconnects computers in a limited area (less than 1 km) such as a home, school, computer laboratory, or office building using network media.
- LAN is a group of computes and associated devices that share a common communication line or wireless link.
- LANs are capable of transmitting data at very fast rates, much faster than data can be transmitted over a telephone line; but the distances are limited, and there is also a limit on the number of computers that can be attached to a single LAN.
- LAN have data rate 10 to 100 Mbps.

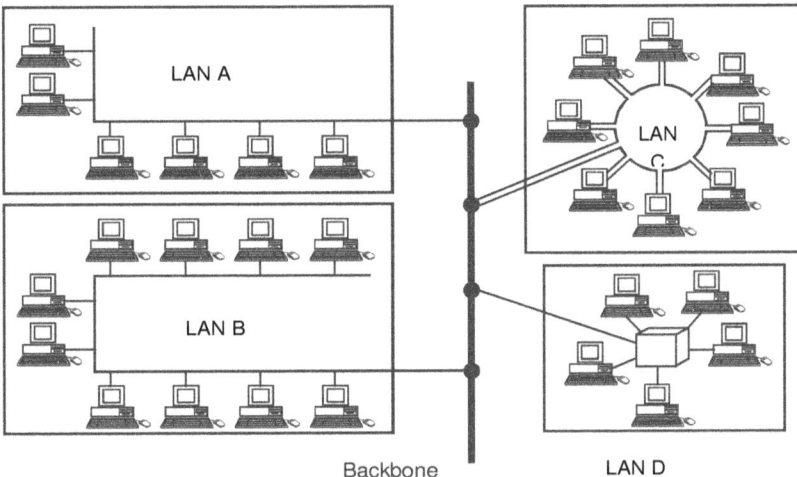

Fig. 3.4: Multiple building LAN (within 1 km distance)

Characteristics of LAN:
1. Every computer has the potential to communicate with any other computers of the network.
2. High degree of interconnection between computers.
3. Easy physical connection of computers in a network.
4. Inexpensive medium of data transmission.
5. High data transmission rate.

Components of a LAN:
1. **Network devices** such as workstations, printers, file servers which are normally accessed by all other computers.
2. **Network Communication Devices** i.e., devices such as hubs, routers, switches etc. used for network connectivity.
3. **Network Interface Cards (NICs)** for each network device required to access the network. It is the interface between the machine and the physical network.
4. **Cable** as a physical transmission medium.
5. **Network Operating System:** Software applications required to control the use of network operation and administration.

Advantages of LANs:
1. Expensive hardware can be shared e.g. laser printers.
2. Network software is cheaper than buying individual packages.
3. Users can access the same files.
4. Messages can be sent between users.
5. A single internet connection can be shared among many users.

Disadvantages of LANs:
1. Quite expensive to set up and maintain.
2. A virus can be easily spread to all the computers on the network.
3. More prone to hacking because of multiple points of access.
4. If the file server goes down, the entire network may go down (star network).
5. Distance and number of computers in a LAN is limited.

Uses of LAN:
1. File transfers and access.
2. Word and text processing.
3. Electronic message handling.
4. Remote database access.
5. Personal computing.
6. Digital voice transmission and storage.

3.3.2 Wide Area Network (WAN)

- WAN is a network that connects users across large distances, often crossing the geographical boundaries of cities or states.
- A WAN provides long-distance transmission of data, voice, image, and video information over large geographical areas that may comprise a country, or even whole world.
- It is geographically distributed network composed of Local Area Networks (LANs) joined into a single large network using services provided by common carriers.
- Wide area networks are commonly implemented in enterprise networking environments in which company offices are in different cities, states, or countries or on different continents.
- WANs often connect multiple smaller networks, such as Local Area Networks (LANs) or Metropolitan Area Networks (MANs).

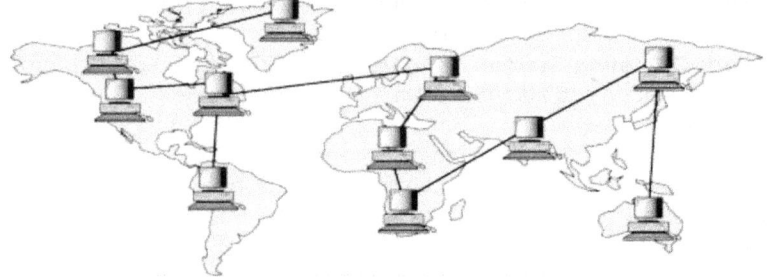

Fig. 3.5: WAN

Characteristics of WAN:
1. It generally covers large distances (states, countries, continents).
2. Communication medium used are satellite, public telephone networks which are connected by routers.
3. Routers forward packets from one to another a route from the sender to the receiver.

Advantages of WAN:
1. WAN covers a large geographical area so long distance businesses can connect on the one network.
2. WAN shares software and resources with connecting workstations.
3. Messages can be sent very quickly to anyone else on the network. These messages can have pictures, sounds, or data included with them (called attachments).
4. Expensive things (such as printers or phone lines to the internet) can be shared by all the computers on the network without having to buy a different peripheral for each computer.
5. Everyone on the network can use the same data. This avoids problems where some users may have older information than others.

Disadvantages of WAN:
1. WANs are expensive and generally slow.
2. WANs need a good firewall to restrict outsiders from entering and disrupting the network.
3. Setting up a network can be an expensive and complicated experience. The bigger the network the more expensive it is.
4. Security is a real issue when many different people have the ability to use information from other computers. Protection against hackers and viruses adds more complexity and expense.

Difference between LAN and WAN:

Terms	LAN	WAN
1. Definition	LAN (Local Area Network) is a computer network covering a small geographic area, like a home, office, schools, or group of buildings.	WAN (Wide Area Network) is a computer network that covers a broad area (e.g., any network whose communications links cross metropolitan, regional, or national boundaries over a long distance.
2. Speed	High speed (1000mbps).	Less speed (150mbps).

contd. ...

3.	Data transfer rates	LANs have a high data transfer rate.	WANs have a lower data transfer rate as compared to LANs.
4.	Example	Network in an organization can be a LAN.	Internet is a good example of a WAN.
5.	Technology	Tend to use certain connectivity, technologies, primarily Ethernet and Token Ring.	WANs tend to use technology like MPLS, ATM, Frame Relay and X.25 for connectivity over the longer distances.
6.	Connection	One LAN can be connected to other LANs over any distance via telephone lines and radio waves.	Computers connected to a wide-area network are often connected through public networks, such as the telephone system. They can also be connected through leased lines or satellites.
7.	Components	Layer 2 devices like switches, bridges. Layer1 devices like hubs, repeaters.	Layers 3 devices Routers, Multi-layer Switches and Technology specific devices like ATM or Frame-relay Switches etc.
8.	Fault Tolerance	LANs tend to have fewer problems associated with them, as there are a smaller amount of systems to deal with.	WANs tend to be less fault tolerant. As it consists of a large amount of systems there is a lower amount of fault tolerance.
9.	Data Transmission Error	Experiences fewer data transmission errors.	Experiences more data transmission errors as compared to LAN.
10.	Ownership	Typically owned, controlled, and managed by a single person or organization.	WANs (like the Internet) are not owned by any one organization but rather exist under collective or distributed ownership and management over long distances.
11.	Set-up costs	If there is a need to set-up a couple of extra devices on the network, it is not very expensive to do that.	In this case since networks in remote areas have to be connected hence the set-up costs are higher. However WANs using public networks can be setup very cheaply.

contd. ...

12. Geographical Spread	Have a small geographical range and do not need any leased telecommunication lines. LAN covers 100 m.	Have a large geographical range generally spreading across boundaries and need leased telecommunication lines. Wan covers more than 100 m.
13. Maintenance costs	Because it covers a relatively small geographical area, LAN is easier to maintain at relatively low costs.	Maintaining WAN is difficult because of its wider geographical coverage and higher maintenance costs.
14. Bandwidth	High bandwidth is available for transmission.	Low bandwidth is available for transmission.

3.3.3 Metropolitan Area Network (MAN)

- Large computer networks that typically span a large city or campus are called Metropolitan Area Networks (MAN).
- MANs geographic scope falls between WAN and LAN.
- MANs provide internet connectivity for LANs in a metropolitan region and connect them to wider area networks like the internet.
- MAN is a public, high-speed network, capable of voice and data transmission over a distance of up to 80 kilometers (50 miles).
- A MAN is smaller than a Wide Area Network (WAN) but larger than a Local Area Network (LAN).
- MAN is designed to extend over an entire city. Multiple Local Area Networks (LANs) that are connected on a campus or industrial complex using a high-speed backbone.
- Multiple networks that are connected within the same city to form a citywide network for a specific government or industry. Any network bigger than a LAN but smaller than a Wide Area Network (WAN) is called as MAN.
- Fiber Distributed Data Interface (FDDI) is a good network technology for building a Metropolitan Area Network (MAN).
- A MAN may be wholly owned and operated by a private company. Number of LANs are connected so that resources may be shared LAN-to-LAN as well as device-to-device. For example: Cable television network.

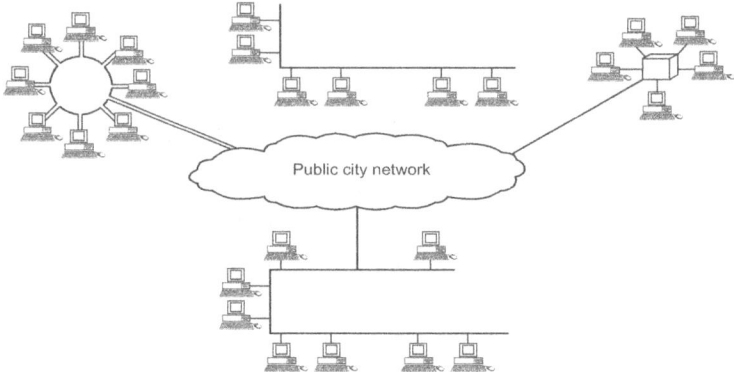

Fig. 3.6: MAN

Characteristics of MAN:
1. It generally covers towns and cities (50 kms).
2. Communication medium used for MAN are optical fibers, cables etc.
3. Data rates adequate for distributed computing applications.

Advantages:
1. MAN spans large geographical area than LAN.
2. MAN falls in between the LAN and WAN therefore, increases the efficiency of handling data. While at the same time saves the cost attached to establish a wide area network.
3. MAN offers centralized management of data. It enables you to connect many fast LANs together.

Logical Classification of Network:
- A network can be divided into two categories:
    1. **Peer-to-Peer Network:** A peer-to-peer network has no dedicated servers. Here a number of workstations are connected together for the purpose of sharing information or devices. All the workstations are considered as equal. Any one computer can act as client or server at any instance. This network is ideal for small networks where there is no need for dedicated servers, like home network or small business establishments or shops. The Microsoft term for peer-to-peer network is "Workgroup". Typically a workgroup contain less than 10 workstations. Normal workstation operating systems are Windows 95/98, ME, XP, NT Workstation, 2000 professional, Vista, RHEL Workstation etc.
    2. **Client-Server:** The client/server model consists of high-end servers serving clients continuously on a network, by providing them with specific services upon request.

3.4 Network Topology

- In computer networking, topology refers to the layout of connected devices.
- Network topology is the study of the arrangement or mapping of the elements (links, nodes, etc.) of a network interconnection between the nodes.
- Topology also determines the strategy for physically expanding the network, in future Topologies can be physical or logical.
- **Physical Topology** means the physical design of a network including the devices, location and cable installation.
- **Logical Topology** refers to the fact that how data actually is transferred in a network as opposed to its design.
- A network topology is the physical layout of computers, cables, and other components on a network. There are a number of different network topologies, and a network may be built using multiple topologies.
- The different types of network layouts are Bus topology, Star topology, Mesh topology, Ring topology, Tree topology and Hybrid topology.

3.4.1 Bus Topology

- In bus topology all devices are connected to a central cable, called the bus or backbone. Bus networks are relatively inexpensive and easy to install for small networks. Ethernet systems use a bus topology.
- A bus topology consists of a main run of cable with a terminator at each end. All nodes like workstations, printers, laptops servers etc., are connected to the linear cable.
- The terminator is used to absorb the signal when the signal reaches the end, preventing signal bounce. When using bus topology, when a computer sends out a signal, the signal travels the cable length in both directions from the sending computer.
- When the signal reaches the end of the cable length, it bounces back and returns in the direction it came from. This is known as signal bounce.
- Signal bounce will create problem in network, because if another signal is sent on the cable length at the same time, the two signals will collide.

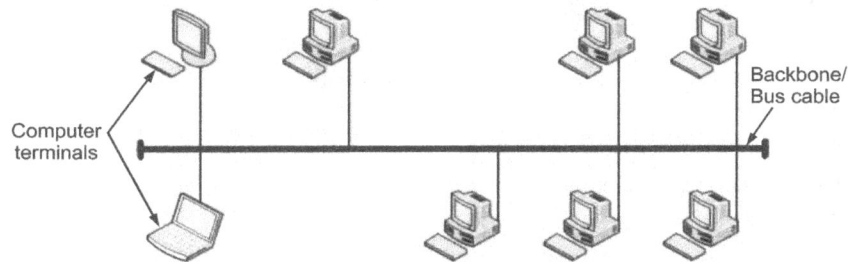

Fig. 3.7: Bus topology

Advantages:
1. Easy to connect a computer or peripheral to a linear bus.
2. Requires less cable length than a star topology.
3. Any computer or device being down does not affect the others.
4. Easy to install.

Disadvantages:
1. Entire network shuts down if there is a break down in the main cable.
2. Terminators are required at both ends of the backbone cable.
3. Difficult to identify the problem if the entire network shuts down.
4. Not meant to be used as a stand-alone solution.

3.4.2 Star Topology

- In start topology all devices are connected to a central hub or switch. Star networks are relatively easy to install and manage, but bottlenecks can occur because all data must pass through the hub or switch.
- A star topology is designed with each node (like workstations, printers, laptops servers etc.,) connected directly to a central network hub/switch. Each workstation has a cable that goes from the network card to network hub or switch.

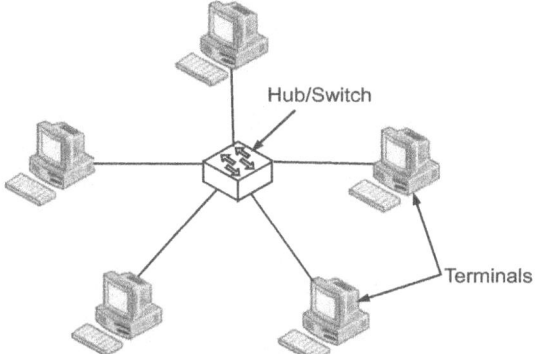

Fig. 3.8: Star topology

Advantages:
1. Easy to install and wire.
2. No disruptions to the network than connecting or removing devices.
3. Easy to detect faults and to remove parts.
4. Eliminates network traffic problem.
5. If one link fails only that link is affected i.e. robustness.

Disadvantages:
1. Requires more cable length than a linear topology.
2. If the hub fails, nodes attached are disabled.
3. More expensive than linear bus topologies because of the cost of the devices.
4. Extra cost of switch.

3.4.3 Ring Topology

- In a ring topology, all computers are connected via a cable that loops in a ring or circle.
- A ring topology is a circle that has no start and no end and terminators are not necessary in a ring topology. Signals travel in one direction on a ring while they are passed from one computer to the next. With each computer the signal is generated so that it can travel the distance required.
- Main advantage of Ring topology is that the signal degeneration is low since each workstation participating in the network is responsible for regenerating the weak signal. Disadvantage is if one workstation fails, entire network will fail.

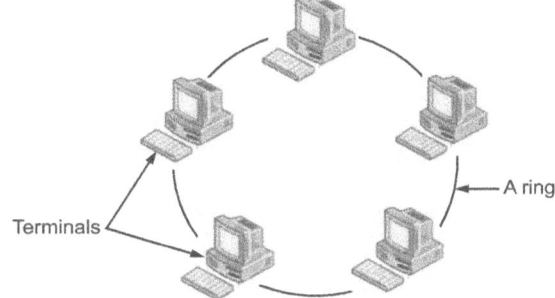

Fig. 3.9: Ring topology

Advantages:
1. Requires less cabling.
2. Less expensive.
3. Fault isolation is simplified.

Disadvantages:
1. Traffic is unidirectional.
2. If one node goes down, it takes down the whole network.
3. Slow in speed.
4. Reconfiguration to add one node, whole network must be down first.
5. Difficult for troubleshooting the ring.

3.4.4 Mesh Topology

- Each device in mesh topology has a dedicated point-to-point link to every other device. The mesh topology connects each computer on the network to the others.
- Fully connected mesh network has $n(n-1)/2$ links for n devices. To accommodate $n(n-1)/2$ links, every device on the network must have $n-1$ input/output (I/O) ports.
- Mesh topology uses a significantly larger amount of network cabling than do the other network topologies, which makes it more expensive.

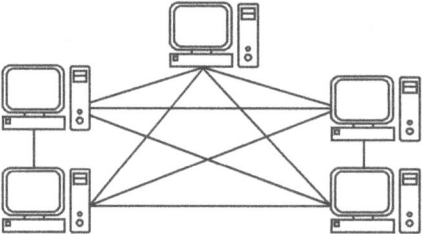

Fig. 3.10: Mesh topology

- In mesh topology, every network device is connected to other network devices. Mesh topology is costly because of the extra cables needed and it is very complex and difficult to manage.
- The mesh topology is highly fault tolerant i.e. every computer has multiple possible connection paths to the other computers on the network, so a single cable break will not stop network communications between any two computers.
- Multiple links to each device are used to provide network link redundancy.
- In most practices networks that are based upon the particularly connected topology, all of the data is transmitted between nodes in network.

Advantages:
1. Each connection can carry its own data load due to dedicated link.
2. Eliminates traffic problem.
3. Mesh topology is robust. If one link becomes unusable, it does not affect other systems.
4. Privacy or Security because of dedicated line.
5. Point-to-point link make fault identification easy.

Disadvantages:
1. More cables are required than other topologies.
2. n–1 Input/Output ports are required for n devices.
3. Installation and reconfiguration is very difficult because each device must be connected to every other device.
4. Expensive due to hardware requirements such as cables and input/output ports.

3.4.5 Tree Topology

- A tree topology is variation of a star topology. In tree topology not every device plugs to the central hub.
- The majority of devices connect to a secondary hub that in turn is connected to the central hub.
- A tree topology can also combine characteristics of linear bus and star topologies. It consists of groups of star-configured workstations connected to a linear bus backbone cable.
- Tree topologies allow for the expansion of an existing network and enable schools to configure a network to meet their needs.

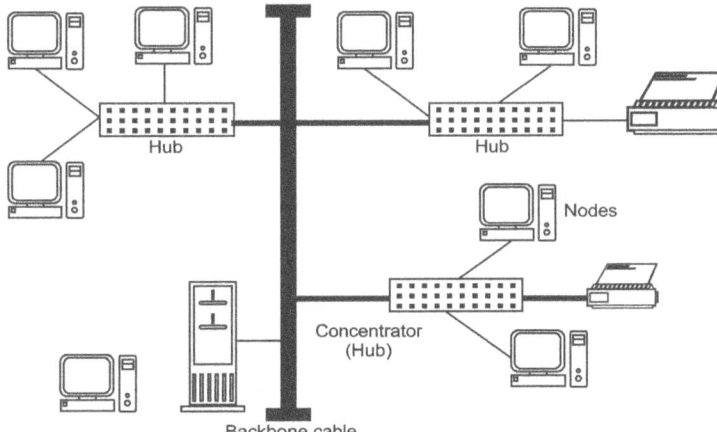

Fig. 3.11: Tree topology

Advantages:
1. Easy to install and wire.
2. Fast as compare to other topologies.
3. Multiple devices can transfer data without collision.
4. Eliminates traffic problem.
5. No disruptions to the network by connecting or removing devices.
6. Easy to detect faults and to remove parts.
7. Supported by several hardware and software vendors.

Disadvantages:
1. If central node (hub) goes down the entire network goes down.
2. Increases the distance of a signal can travel between network devices.
3. More expensive than bus topologies because of the cost of the concentrators (hub or switch).
4. The cabling cost is more.

3.3.6 Hybrid Topology

- A hybrid topology is combination of two or more network topologies. Fig. 3.18 shows a hybrid star and bus topologies.
- Hybrid topology is a mixture or combination of topologies to implement a network.
- A very common and popular hybrid topology is star-bus topology in which a number of star topologies and bus topologies are connected by a central hub or switch.
- This topology is popular because the bus will connect hubs that are spread over distances.
- In this topology, if a computer fails, it will not affect the rest of the network. However, if the central component or hub, that attaches all computers in a star, fails, then you have big problems since no computer will be able to communicate.

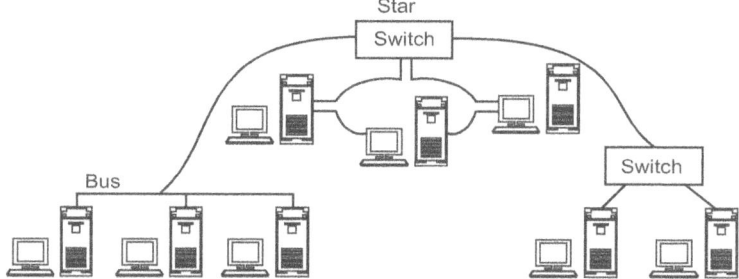

Fig. 3.12: Hybrid topology (starbus)

Advantages:
1. Network expansion is very simple in case of hybrid technology.
2. If one client fails, the entire network does not fail.

Disadvantage:
1. If one hub fails, all connections to that hub fail, although other hubs continue to function.

3.5 Current Trends in IT Management

- 'When you've got 300 million people on Facebook, that's a huge business watering hole,' says Lon Safko, social media expert and co-author of *The Social Media Bible: Tactics, Tools, and Strategies for Business Success*, of the site's global reach. 'The profile is like an index to your company.'
- While Facebook has become the most popular social media site, there are plenty of others for your company to explore. LinkedIn, for example, houses 55 million professionals seeking jobs, employees, or basic business or networking opportunities. MySpace, which allows users to tinker with music, themes, and HTML code, is targeted toward youth and teens. All of these sites have one primary thing in common: the profile.

- The user profile is generally what distinguishes social networking sites from other social media platforms. It helps set the stage for building relationships with people who share the same interests, activities, or personal contacts, as opposed to primarily disseminating or digesting information feeds. This also means social networks enable companies to invite audiences to get to know its brand in a way that traditional forms of marketing or advertising can't.
- But what, exactly, are the methods that businesses should use to effectively leverage the burgeoning userbase of these sites as a tool to grow their companies? The following pages will detail what to do – and what not to do – in order to maintain a viable presence in the realm of social networking.

3.5.1 How to Use Social Networking Sites to Drive Business: Developing a Social Networking Strategy

- Before opening an account and becoming active, it's important to consider what each site offers and how you can benefit from their resources. 'Take some time and really analyze what your existing social media strategy is,' says Safko. 'Figure out which tools are best for your demographic.' Without a fully developed plan for your social networking activity, you could end up meandering throughout the sites and wasting a lot of time.
- Here are a few basic questions to ask yourself when forming your social networking strategy:
  1. **What are the needs of my business?** Hopefully, you're not putting your company name on a social networking account just to send messages back and forth to former high school classmates, so there has to be an impetus. Figure out what your needs are. Are you short-staffed? Is your advertising budget running thin?
  2. **What am I using the site for?** After you've established your needs, consider the primary goal of your social networking strategy. Do you want to recruit employees for a certain department? Do you want to market a new line of products? Do you want to connect to more people in your industry?
  3. **Whose attention am I trying to get?** Okay, so you want to market that new line of products, for example. You still need to know your target audience for that product, and with more than 300 million users on Facebook, you'll need to narrow your focus.
  4. **Which sites do I want to take on?** If you have enough staffing power to handle multiple social networking sites, that's great. If not, it's important to focus on one or two, or you could spread yourself too thin and fall victim to the 'gaping void' perception, where you end up going days without activity. Your followers will notice.

5. **Who's going to manage my page?** Would your social networking activity fall under a current employee's responsibilities, or do you need to bring on new talent? If you ever find yourself without the staffing resources to manage your page, don't stick your head in the sand, says Safko. 'Find some interns,' he advises. 'In most cases, they'll do it for free.'
6. **Who has access to my page?** What type of trust level do you have established at your company? Will all of your employees have access to the social network account, or a select few? Take the time to assess the skills and character of those who can log into your page, or you may run into unsavory situations down the road – especially when dealing with former workers.
7. **Who's going to be the personality of my page?** Does your company already have a public representative that usually handles speeches, press, etc.? It may be beneficial to rein in that person as the voice of your social networking site. 'People buy from other people, not from other companies,' says Safko. 'In order to solidify trust, pick someone to represent your brand.'

3.5.2 How to Use Social Networking Sites to Drive Business: Choosing Your Site

- After you've answered those questions, you can choose which social networking site, or sites, would best fulfill the requirements of your strategy. Though many of the sites are similar in nature, they can all be categorized by the different purposes they serve. These are the basic types of social networking sites:

    1. **'Free for all' social sites:** Some sites that fall under this category are Facebook, MySpace,Ning, and Friendster. Each of these sites primarily serve as a nexus of friends and associates who want to socialize. Ning, for example, has become popular for connecting classmates and helping to set up reunions. The profiles are usually personable, inviting, and can be customized with add-ons and apps.
    2. **Professional sites:** Examples of these include LinkedIn, FastPitch, and Plaxo. The professional site can be utilized as an online professional contact database, or 'rolodex,' but it's also where people go to update employment information about themselves.
    3. **Industry-specific sites:** These sites allow you to connect to people who are in your industry.I-Meet, for example, is specifically geared toward event planners, while ResearchGATE is a community for researchers in the science or technology field. Industry sites help you to narrow your search when looking for services, or people with skills in certain fields. You may even want a particular department of your company, such as IT or advertising, to open an account on one of these sites.

3.5.3 How to Use Social Networking Sites to Drive Business: Setting Up Your Profile

- Your profile is the online representation of your brand and company, so it's important to know what to add and what to avoid. Here are a few tips to be mindful of as you create your profile:
    1. **Don't be afraid to get a little personal:** Facebook profiles, for example, allow you to include things like hobbies, favorite music, etc. Including tidbits like these can make your page warmer and more personable. 'Some personal information is valuable, because it may create a bond with a customer,' says Safko.
    2. **But not too personal:** Don't be the 'TMI' poster boy or girl, (i.e. 'The wife and I are on our way to have dinner – kids are with the grandparents'). Create another page that's just yours, sans company activity.
    3. **Share photos and videos:** Adding multimedia to your page gives flair, and offers customers an exclusive look inside your company. LinkedIn even has an add-on that allows you to post presentations and slideshows.
    4. **But no office party snapshots:** Though the atmosphere of Facebook is still relatively laid back, you want to maintain the perception that you're serious about your product and customers. Pictures involving Santa hats and alcohol probably shouldn't be in your albums.
    5. **Set privacy settings:** On most of these sites, you can control what people see on your profile, such as pictures and blog posts, and you can even limit what other people post. Depending on the nature of your company, you should consider these restrictions. Are there any embarrassing pictures of you floating around that you might not want linked to your page?
    6. **But don't be a blank slate:** Imagine coming across the profile of one your favorite brands, and all that's there is a picture and headquarters location. A little disheartening, right? If and when you do enact some privacy settings, try to keep the page lively.

3.5.4 How to Use Social Networking Sites to Drive Business: Social Network Marketing

- Marketing through social networks isn't as much about selling your product, as it is about engaging your followers. 'A lot of people have started Facebook fan pages with no clue to how it can benefit them,' says Jim Tobin, president of Ignite Social Media, a social media marketing agency based in Cary, North Carolina. 'You have to think above your product.' The goal of the community-based environment of social networking sites is to provide a platform for an open, honest conversation.
- The companies that are most successful at converting followers into dollars are those who interact most with the users and frequently post content related to their brand.

Facebook'sFan Page is probably the best example of how you should be marketing you company through social networking sites. The page acts as an upgraded user profile for brands, companies, and organizations to be as involved as the users, and has plenty of tools to help you do so. As users become 'fans' of your page, all of your activity appears in their News Feed each time they log on. There's also a useful feature called the Insights tool, which allows you to analyze page views, the demographics of your fans, and the number of people who view (or stop viewing) your News Feed posts.

- Outdoor Technology, a Los Angeles-based manufacturer of clothing and gear for skiers and snowboarders, initially sold merchandise directly to retailers. But after the company began actively using their Fan Page last September, revenue from e-commerce went from zero to $25,000 in three months, says CEO Caro Krissman. The page has now amassed over 11,000 fans. 'We saw Facebook as sort of a sweet spot for where our target market is,' says Krissman. 'With the ability to target users in such a focused way, we felt like there really wasn't a better forum to go about [marketing online].'

'Fan' features your company should be using:

1. **Comment on other users' content or profile posts:** By responding to what your followers post to your profile, you show them that you appreciate their interaction. If they know they have your attention, they'll keep coming back.
2. **Ask questions on your wall:** Facebook users love to be heard. It can be surprising how many responses one question can elicit. 'It starts to snowball,' says Safko. 'What you'll find is that the conversation will branch off and start another one.'
3. **Posting links or threads:** 'One thing fan pages lets you do that Web pages don't is encourage viral spread,' says Tobin. If you have any content that you want to circulate quickly, the fan page is the perfect tool.
4. **Posting relevant events:** By posting upcoming events your company may be part of or hosting, you can help drive more attendees to the function. And for those who can't come, they get a glimpse at how active your business is within the community or industry.

3.5.5 Social Network Promotions

- Remember, it's called a social network, not a 'business network.' Coming off as a pushy or shrewd salesperson peddling a product could scare away your Facebook friends and LinkedIn connections. Remember to be genuine and personal.
- Here are the things you should do when promoting your company or product through social networking sites:
    1. **Make it benefit-based:** Make the customer feel that they need to participate in the promotion. Is the product or feature available for a limited time? Are you offering exclusively to your followers on a particular network?

2. **Talk about new or uncommon features:** Even if you have a relatively popular product, there may be some things consumers don't know about it. What are some new or different ways it can be used?
3. **Include some discounts and savings:** Offering discounts on products is usually a shoe-in to grab customers' attention. Krissman, of Outdoor Technology, says he posts promotional codes that users can fill out on the company's website and get up to 30 percent off a product. Not only does it drive more buyers to your product, but it also brings more followers to your page.

- Here are the things you shouldn't do when promoting your company or product through social networking sites:
  1. **Don't continually have sales-related messages:** There are other ways to promote besides selling your product. Comment or ask questions about news or topics in your industry. 'They will easily ignore you or unsubscribe you if you continue to push a sale,' says Tobin.
  2. **Don't set up an expectation, then cheat on it:** If you announce to your followers that your purpose is to give advice, don't turn around and start selling. 'If you violate that expectation, people are going to get upset and they're going to leave,' says Tobin. Again, make the sale subtle – how can your product help them achieve the advice you're giving?

3.5.6 How to Use Social Networking Sites to Drive Business: Social Network Recruiting

- Social recruiting is an effective way to utilize social networks to find the best candidate for any open positions at your company. While the past few years saw the rise of job boards like Careerbuilder.com and Monster.com, the growing prominence of social networks have transformed the way businesses build their best team. Instead of relying on the 'come one, come all' approach, the detailed personal information contained in profiles, such as interests and job history, allows businesses to employ social networking sites to target the specific audience or skill set they want to pull from.
- According to an annual social recruitment survey published by Jobvite, an online service that helps businesses consolidate the resources of social media sites, 80 percent of companies used or planned to use social networking to find and attract candidates in 2009, with LinkedIn being used by 95 percent of the respondents and Facebook usage growing from 36 percent in 2008 to 59 percent in 2009.
- 'It's like what's happened to the ad industry,' says Dan Finnigan, CEO of Jobvite and former general manager of Yahoo! HotJobs. 'It used to be that you would buy a big ad to get the consumer's attention, but more and more companies are relying on online advertising software that puts that ad right in front of them based on data, like the other ads they click on. Social recruiting is analogous to that.'

3.5.7 The Benefits of Social Network Recruiting

- Here are some of the primary advantages that social recruiting affords small businesses:
    1. **Empowers your employees to distribute job information.** These days, most, if not all of your employees probably have a profile on a social networking site. By enabling them to post information about open positions, you multiply your searching reach by the thousands.
    2. **Helps you put the passive job candidate in your crosshairs:** Job boards are mostly used by people who are proactively looking for positions. But what about the perfect potential employee who may not be scouring Careerbuilder.com every day?
    3. **A low-cost method of finding high-quality candidates:** When looking for job candidates, it takes time to sift through resumes of unqualified applicants, and many job boards charge fees to post openings. Social recruiting helps you zone in on the best candidates, for free.

Tools to Help You Socially Recruit
1. **Custom searches:** Searching only by name and location doesn't cut it when looking for the perfect employee. LinkedIn has one of the most thorough searches of all the sites, allowing you to sift through profiles by company, industry, college, and even how many 'degrees' you are from the person.
2. **Updating your status message:** When you or your employees update your statuses, it pops up on your friends' home page, and sits atop the profile until it's changed. 'My company is looking for ... ,' is sure to snag replies.
3. **Linking to stories and external content:** Both Facebook and LinkedIn enable users to post external content to their profiles. By linking to articles and blogs that contain positive news about your business, you show potential candidates that it's not just your social network connections that adore your company.

How to Use Social Networking Sites to Drive Business: Privacy and Legal Issues

- Though social networking can certainly be a fun way to help you expand your company, there are plenty of issues surrounding privacy and legalities that you should always be aware of when searching for employees, and even after you've hired them. 'The laws apply the same,' says Megan Erickson, an associate at Des Moines, Iowa-based Dickinson, Mackaman, Tyler & Hagan law firm and author of Erickson's Blog on Social Networking and the Law. 'But now that there are all these different kinds of social media, they combine to make it a very unique environment.'
- Here are some of the most important things to keep in mind to help you steer clear of legal trouble when dealing with potential or current employees and social networking sites:

1. **Don't use fake profiles:** Using a fake profile when adding employees to monitor their activity can constitute as an invasion of privacy, Erickson says. 'That's just asking for lots of trouble,' she says.
2. **Add a social media section to your handbook:** Including language about social media in your personnel policy is paramount, especially if you plan on integrating it heavily in your company's operations.
3. **Beware of existing federal and state laws:** It may help to prep yourself on the many federal and state laws regarding anti-discrimination and privacy, Erickson says, so that if you do come across an employee's wayward photo or disparaging status message, you'll be knowledgeable about how to proceed with disciplinary action.

3.6 ICT applications: benefits in all aspects of life

- ICT applications can support sustainable development, in the fields of public administration, business, education and training, health, employment, environment, agriculture and science within the framework of national e-strategies. This would include actions within the following sectors:

1. **E-government:**
    1. Implement e-government strategies focusing on applications aimed at innovating and promoting transparency in public administrations and democratic processes, improving efficiency and strengthening relations with citizens.
    2. Develop national e-government initiatives and services, at all levels, adapted to the needs of citizens and business, to achieve a more efficient allocation of resources and public goods.
    3. Support international cooperation initiatives in the field of e-government, in order to enhance transparency, accountability and efficiency at all levels of government.
2. **E-business:**
    1. Governments, international organizations and the private sector, are encouraged to promote the benefits of international trade and the use of e-business, and promote the use of e-business models in developing countries and countries with economies in transition.
    2. Through the adoption of an enabling environment, and based on widely available Internet access, governments should seek to stimulate private sector investment, foster new applications, content development and public/private partnerships.
    3. Government policies should favour assistance to, and growth of SMMEs, in the ICT industry, as well as their entry into e-business, to stimulate economic growth and job creation as an element of a strategy for poverty reduction through wealth creation.

3. E-Learning (See Section C4):

- Everyone should have the necessary skills to benefit fully from the Information Society. Therefore capacity building and ICT literacy are essential. ICTs can contribute to achieving universal education worldwide, through delivery of education and training of teachers, and offering improved conditions for lifelong learning, encompassing people that are outside the formal education process, and improving professional skills.
    1. Develop domestic policies to ensure that ICTs are fully integrated in education and training at all levels, including in curriculum development, teacher training, institutional administration and management, and in support of the concept of lifelong learning.
    2. Develop and promote programmes to eradicate illiteracy using ICTs at national, regional and international levels.
    3. Promote e-literacy skills for all, for example by designing and offering courses for public administration, taking advantage of existing facilities such as libraries, multipurpose community centres, public access points and by establishing local ICT training centres with the cooperation of all stakeholders. Special attention should be paid to disadvantaged and vulnerable groups.
    4. In the context of national educational policies, and taking into account the need to eradicate adult illiteracy, ensure that young people are equipped with knowledge and skills to use ICTs, including the capacity to analyse and treat information in creative and innovative ways, share their expertise and participate fully in the Information Society.
    5. Governments, in cooperation with other stakeholders, should create programmes for capacity building with an emphasis on creating a critical mass of qualified and skilled ICT professionals and experts.
    6. Develop pilot projects to demonstrate the impact of ICT-based alternative educational delivery systems, notably for achieving Education for All targets, including basic literacy targets.
    7. Work on removing the gender barriers to ICT education and training and promoting equal training opportunities in ICT-related fields for women and girls. Early intervention programmes in science and technology should target young girls with the aim of increasing the number of women in ICT careers. Promote the exchange of best practices on the integration of gender perspectives in ICT education.
    8. Empower local communities, especially those in rural and underserved areas, in ICT use and promote the production of useful and socially meaningful content for the benefit of all.

9. Launch education and training programmes, where possible using information networks of traditional nomadic and indigenous peoples, which provide opportunities to fully participate in the Information Society.
10. Design and implement regional and international cooperation activities to enhance the capacity, notably, of leaders and operational staff in developing countries and LDCs, to apply ICTs effectively in the whole range of educational activities. This should include delivery of education outside the educational structure, such as the workplace and at home.
11. Design specific training programmes in the use of ICTs in order to meet the educational needs of information professionals, such as archivists, librarians, museum professionals, scientists, teachers, journalists, postal workers and other relevant professional groups. Training of information professionals should focus not only on new methods and techniques for the development and provision of information and communication services, but also on relevant management skills to ensure the best use of technologies. Training of teachers should focus on the technical aspects of ICTs, on development of content, and on the potential possibilities and challenges of ICTs.
12. Develop distance learning, training and other forms of education and training as part of capacity building programmes. Give special attention to developing countries and especially LDCs in different levels of human resources development.
13. Promote international and regional cooperation in the field of capacity building, including country programmes developed by the United Nations and its Specialized Agencies.
14. Launch pilot projects to design new forms of ICT-based networking, linking education, training and research institutions between and among developed and developing countries and countries with economies in transition.
15. Volunteering, if conducted in harmony with national policies and local cultures, can be a valuable asset for raising human capacity to make productive use of ICT tools and build a more inclusive Information Society. Activate volunteer programmes to provide capacity building on ICT for development, particularly in developing countries.
16. Design programmes to train users to develop self-learning and self-development capacities.

4. **E-health:**
   1. Promote collaborative efforts of governments, planners, health professionals, and other agencies along with the participation of international organizations for creating a reliable, timely, high quality and affordable health care and health information systems and for promoting continuous medical training, education, and research through the use of ICTs, while respecting and protecting citizens' right to privacy.

2. Facilitate access to the world's medical knowledge and locally-relevant content resources for strengthening public health research and prevention programmes and promoting women's and men's health, such as content on sexual and reproductive health and sexually transmitted infections, and for diseases that attract full attention of the world including HIV/AIDS, malaria and tuberculosis.
3. Alert, monitor and control the spread of communicable diseases, through the improvement of common information systems.
4. Promote the development of international standards for the exchange of health data, taking due account of privacy concerns.
5. Encourage the adoption of ICTs to improve and extend health care and health information systems to remote and underserved areas and vulnerable populations, recognising women's roles as health providers in their families and communities.
6. Strengthen and expand ICT-based initiatives for providing medical and humanitarian assistance in disasters and emergencies.

5. **E-employment:**
   1. Encourage the development of best practices for e-workers and e-employers built, at the national level, on principles of fairness and gender equality, respecting all relevant international norms.
   2. Promote new ways of organizing work and business with the aim of raising productivity, growth and well-being through investment in ICTs and human resources.
   3. Promote teleworking to allow citizens, particularly in the developing countries, LDCs, and small economies, to live in their societies and work anywhere, and to increase employment opportunities for women, and for those with disabilities. In promoting teleworking, special attention should be given to strategies promoting job creation and the retention of the skilled working force.
   4. Promote early intervention programmes in science and technology that should target young girls to increase the number of women in ICT carriers.

6. **E-environment**
   1. Governments, in cooperation with other stakeholders are encouraged to use and promote ICTs as an instrument for environmental protection and the sustainable use of natural resources.
   2. Government, civil society and the private sector are encouraged to initiate actions and implement projects and programmes for sustainable production and consumption and the environmentally safe disposal and recycling of discarded hardware and components used in ICTs.
   3. Establish monitoring systems, using ICTs, to forecast and monitor the impact of natural and man-made disasters, particularly in developing countries, LDCs and small economies.

7. **E-agriculture**
   1. Ensure the systematic dissemination of information using ICTs on agriculture, animal husbandry, fisheries, forestry and food, in order to provide ready access to comprehensive, up-to-date and detailed knowledge and information, particularly in rural areas.
   2. Public-private partnerships should seek to maximize the use of ICTs as an instrument to improve production (quantity and quality).

8. **E-science**
   1. Promote affordable and reliable high-speed Internet connection for all universities and research institutions to support their critical role in information and knowledge production, education and training, and to support the establishment of partnerships, cooperation and networking between these institutions.
   2. Promote electronic publishing, differential pricing and open access initiatives to make scientific information affordable and accessible in all countries on an equitable basis.
   3. Promote the use of peer-to-peer technology to share scientific knowledge and pre-prints and reprints written by scientific authors who have waived their right to payment.
   4. Promote the long-term systematic and efficient collection, dissemination and preservation of essential scientific digital data, for example, population and meteorological data in all countries.
   5. Promote principles and metadata standards to facilitate cooperation and effective use of collected scientific information and data as appropriate to conduct scientific research.

■■■

Chapter 4...

The Internet and the New Information Technology Infrastructure

Contents ...
4.1 The IT Infrastructure for the Digital Firm
    4.1.1 The Competitive Business Environment and the Emerging Digital Firm
    4.1.2 Emergence of the Global Economy
    4.1.3 Transformation of Industrial Economies
    4.1.4 The Emerging Digital Firm
4.2 Behavioral Approach
    4.2.1 Approach of This Text: Sociotechnical Systems
    4.2.2 The Widening Scope of Information Systems
    4.2.3 The Network Revolution and the Internet
4.3 Learning to Use Information Systems: New Opportunities with Technology
4.4 Overview of World Wide Web (Web Server and Client)
    4.4.1 Definition
    4.4.2 How does the WWW Work?
4.5 Management Issues and Decisions

4.1 The IT Infrastructure for the Digital Firm

Why Information Systems?
- Today it is widely recognized that information systems knowledge is essential for managers because most organizations need information systems to survive and prosper. Information systems can help companies extend their reach to faraway locations, offer new products and services, reshape jobs and work flows, and perhaps profoundly change the way they conduct business.

4.1.1 The Competitive Business Environment and the Emerging Digital Firm

- Four powerful worldwide changes have altered the business environment. The first change is the emergence and strengthening of the global economy. The second change is the transformation of industrial economies and societies into knowledge- and information-based service economies. The third is the transformation of the business enterprise. The fourth is the emergence of the digital firm. These changes in the business environment and climate, summarized in Table 4.1, pose a number of new challenges to business firms and their management.

Table 4.1: The Changing Contemporary Business Environment

Globalization
Management and control in a global
Marketplace
Competition in world markets
Global work groups
Global delivery systems
Transformation of the Enterprise
Flattening
Decentralization
Flexibility
Location independence
Low transaction and coordination
Costs
Empowerment
Collaborative work and teamwork
Transformation of Industrial Economies
Knowledge and information-based
Economies
Productivity
New products and services
Knowledge: a central productive and strategic asset
Time-based competition
Shorter product life
Turbulent environment
Limited employee knowledge base
Emergence of the Digital Firm
Digitally enabled relationships with customers, suppliers, and employees
Core business processes accomplished via digital networks
Digital management of key corporate assets
Rapid sensing and responding to environmental changes

4.1.2 Emergence of the Global Economy

- A growing percentage of the American economy—and other advanced industrial economies in Europe and Asia—depends on imports and exports. Foreign trade, both exports and imports, accounts for more than 25 percent of the goods and services produced in the United States, and even more in countries such as Japanand Germany. Companies are also distributing core business functions in product design, manufacturing, finance, and customer support to locations in other countries where the work can be performed more cost effectively. The success of firms today and in the future depends on their ability to operate globally.

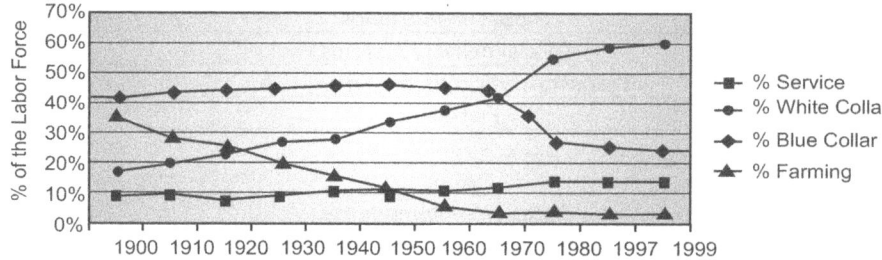

Fig. 4.1: The Growth of the Information Economy

- Since the beginning of the twentieth century, the United States has experienced a steady decline in the number of farm workers and blue-collar workers who are employed in factories. At the same time, the country is experiencing a rise in the number of white-collar workers who produce economic value using knowledge and information.

- Today, information systems provide the communication and analytic power that firms need for conducting trade and managing businesses on a global scale. Controlling the far-flung global corporation— communicating with distributors and suppliers, operating 24 hours a day in different national environments, coordinating global work teams, and servicing local and international reporting needs—is a major business challenge that requires powerful information system responses.

- Globalization and information technology also bring new threats to domestic business firms: Because of global communication and management systems, customers now can shop in a worldwide marketplace, obtaining price and quality information reliably 24 hours a day. To become competitive participants in international markets, firms need powerful information and communication systems.

4.1.3 Transformation of Industrial Economies

- The United States, Japan, Germany, and other major industrial powers are being transformed from industrial economies to knowledge- and information-based service

- economies, whereas manufacturing has been moving to low-wage countries. In a knowledge and information-based economy, knowledge and information are key ingredients in creating wealth.
- The knowledge and information revolution began at the turn of the twentieth century and has gradually accelerated. By 1976 the number of white-collar workers employed in offices surpassed the number of farm workers, service workers, and blue-collar workers employed in manufacturing (see Fig. 4.1. Today, most people no longer work on farms or in factories but instead are found in sales, education, healthcare, banks, insurance firms, and law firms; they also provide business services like copying, computer programming, or making deliveries. These jobs primarily involve working with, distributing, or creating new knowledge and information. In fact, knowledge and information work now account for a significant 60 percent of the American gross national product and nearly 55 percent of the labor force.
- Knowledge and information are becoming the foundation for many new services and products. Knowledge and information-intense products such as computer games require a great deal of knowledge to produce.
- Entire new information-based services have sprung up, such as Lexis, Dow Jones News Service, and America Online. These fields are employing millions of people. Knowledge is used more intensively in the production of traditional products as well. In the automobile industry, for instance, both design and production now rely heavily on knowledge and information technology.
- In a knowledge and information-based economy, information technology and systems take on great importance. Knowledge-based products and services of great economic value, such as credit cards, overnight package delivery, and worldwide reservation systems, are based on new information technologies.
- Information technology constitutes more than 70 percent of the invested capital in service industries such as finance, insurance, and real estate.
- Across all industries, information and the technology that delivers it have become critical, strategic assets for business firms and their managers (Leonard-Barton, 1995). Information systems are needed to optimize the flow of information and knowledge within the organization and to help management maximize the firm's knowledge resources. Because employees' productivity depends on the quality of the systems serving them, management decisions about information technology are critically important to the firm's prosperity and survival.

Transformation of the Business Enterprise
- There has been a transformation in the possibilities for organizing and managing the business enterprise. Some firms have begun to take advantage of these new possibilities.

- The traditional business firm was—and still is—a hierarchical, centralized, structured arrangement of specialists that typically relied on a fixed set of standard operating procedures to deliver a mass-produced product (or service). The new style of business firm is a flattened (less hierarchical), decentralized, flexible arrangement of generalists who rely on nearly instant information to deliver mass-customized products and services uniquely suited to specific markets or customers.
- The traditional management group relied—and still relies—on formal plans, a rigid division of labor, and formal rules. The new manager relies on informal commitments and networks to establish goals (rather than formal planning), a flexible arrangement of teams and individuals working in task forces, and a customer orientation to achieve coordination among employees. The new manager appeals to the knowledge, learning, and decision making of individual employees to ensure proper operation of the firm. Once again, information technology makes this style of management possible.

4.1.4 The Emerging Digital Firm

- The intensive use of information technology in business firms since the mid-1990s, coupled with equally significant organizational redesign, has created the conditions for a new phenomenon in industrial society— the fully digital firm. The digital firm can be defined along several dimensions. A digital firm is one where nearly all of the organization's significant business relationships with customers, suppliers, and employees are digitally enabled and mediated. Core business processes are accomplished through digital networks spanning the entire organization or linking multiple organizations. Business processes refer to the unique manner in which work is organized, coordinated, and focused to produce a valuable product or service.
- Developing a new product, generating and fulfilling an order, or hiring an employee are examples of business processes, and the way organizations accomplish their business processes can be a source of competitive strength. Key corporate assets—intellectual property, core competencies, financial, and human assets—are managed through digital means. In a digital firm, any piece of information required to support key business decisions is available at anytime and anywhere in the firm. Digital firms sense and respond to their environments far more rapidly than traditional firms, giving them more flexibility to survive in turbulent times. Digital firms offer extraordinary opportunities for more global organization and management. By digitally enabling and streamlining their work, digital firms have the potential to achieve unprecedented levels of profitability and competitiveness.
- Digital firms are distinguished from traditional firms by their near total reliance on a set of information technologies to organize and manage. For managers of digital firms, information technology is not simply a useful handmaiden, an enabler, but rather it is the core of the business and the primary management tool.

- There are very few fully digital firms today. Yet nearly all firms—especially larger traditional firms—are being driven in this direction by a number of business forces and opportunities. Despite the recent decline in technology investments and Internet-only businesses, firms are continuing to invest heavily in information systems that integrate internal business processes and build closer links with suppliers and customers. Cisco Systems, described in the chapter ending case study, is close to becoming a fully digital firm, using Internet technology to drive every aspect of its business. Procter & Gamble, described in the chapter opening vignette is another digital firm in the making.
- Moving from a traditional firm foundation toward a digital firm requires insight, skill, and patience. Managers need to identify the challenges facing their firms; discover the technologies that will help them meet these challenges; organize their firms and business processes to take advantage of the technology; and create management procedures and policies to implement the required changes. This book is dedicated to helping managers prepare for these tasks.

What is an Information System?

- An information system can be defined technically as a set of interrelated components that collect, process, store, and distribute information to support decision making, coordination and control in an organization. In addition to supporting decision making, coordination, and control, information systems may also help managers and workers analyze problems, visualize complex subjects, and create new products.
- Information systems contain information about significant people, places, and things within the organization or in the environment surrounding it. By information we mean data that have been shaped into a form that is meaningful and useful to human beings. Data, in contrast, are streams of raw facts representing events occurring in organizations or the physical environment before they have been organized and arranged into a form that people can understand and use.
- A brief example contrasting information to data may prove useful. Supermarket checkout counters ring up millions of pieces of data, such as product identification numbers or the cost of each item sold. Such pieces of data can be totalled and analyzed to provide meaningful information such as the total number of bottles of dish detergent sold at a particular store, which brands of dish detergent were selling the most rapidly at that store or sales territory, or the total amount spent on that brand of dish detergent at that store or sales region (see Fig. 4.2).

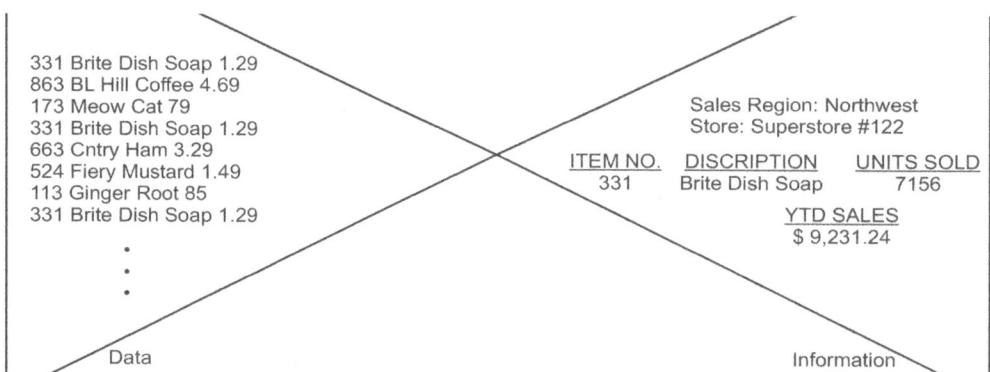

Fig. 4.2: Data and Information

- Raw data from a supermarket checkout counter can be processed and organized in order to produce meaningful information such as the total unit sales of dish detergent or the total sales revenue from dish detergent for a specific store or sales territory.
- Three activities in an information system produce the information that organizations need to make decisions, control operations, analyze problems, and create new products or services. These activities are input, processing, and output (Fig. 4.3). Input captures or collects raw data from within the organization or from its external environment. Processing converts this raw input into a more meaningful form. Output transfers the processed information to the people who will use it or to the activities for which it will be used.
- Information systems also require feedback, which is output that is returned to appropriate members of the organization to help them evaluate or correct the input stage.

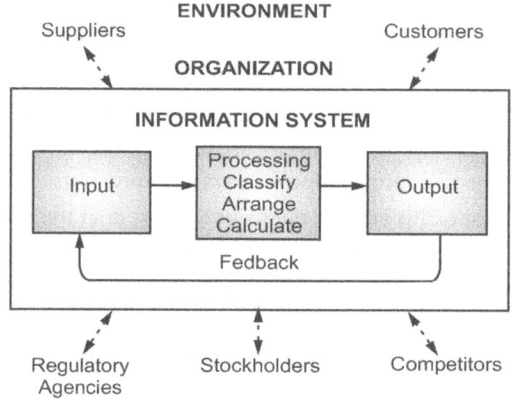

Fig. 4.3: Functions of an information system

- An information system contains information about an organization and its surrounding environment. Three basic activities—input, processing, and output—produce the information organizations need. Feedback is output returned to appropriate people or activities in the organization to evaluate and refine the input. Environmental factors such as customers, suppliers, competitors, stockholders, and regulatory agencies interact with the organization and its information systems.

- In Procter & Gamble's point-of-sale system, the raw input consists of the item identification number, item description, and amount of each item sold along with the retailer's name and identification number. A computer processes these data by comparing the amount of each item sold to the historical sales pattern for that item to determine if the item might soon be out of stock. The system then sends alerts over computers and wireless devices to appropriate store personnel to reorder the item, which become the system outputs.

- The system thus provides meaningful information, such as lists of what retailer ordered what items, the total number of each item ordered daily, the total number of each item ordered by each retailer, and items that need to be restocked.

- Our interest in this book is in formal, organizational computer-based information systems (CBIS) like those designed and used by Procter & Gamble and its customers, suppliers, and employees. Formal systems rest on accepted and fixed definitions of data and procedures for collecting, storing, processing, disseminating, and using these data. The formal systems we describe in this text are structured; that is, they operate in conformity with predefined rules that are relatively fixed and not easily changed. For instance, Procter & Gamble's point-of-sale system requires that all orders include the retailer's name and identification number and a unique number for identifying each item.

- Informal information systems rely, by contrast, on unstated rules of behavior. There is no agreement on what is information, or on how it will be stored and processed. Such systems are essential for the life of an organization, but an analysis of their qualities is beyond the scope of this text.

- Formal information systems can be either computer-based or manual. Manual systems use paper-and-pencil technology. These manual systems serve important needs, but they too are not the subject of this text.

- Computer-based information systems, in contrast, rely on computer hardware and software technology to process and disseminate information. From this point on, when we use the term information systems, we are referring to computer-based information systems—formal organizational systems that rely on computer technology. The Window on Technology describes some of the typical technologies used in computer-based information systems today.

- Although computer-based information systems use computer technology to process raw data into meaningful information, there is a sharp distinction between a computer and a computer program on the one hand, and an information system on the other. Electronic computers and related software programs are the technical foundation, the tools and materials, of modern information systems. Computers provide the equipment for storing and processing information. Computer programs, or software, are sets of operating instructions that direct and control computer processing. Knowing how computers and computer programs work is important in designing solutions to organizational problems, but computers are only part of an information system. A house is an appropriate analogy. Houses are built with hammers, nails, and wood, but these do not make a house. The architecture, design, setting, landscaping, and all of the decisions that lead to the creation of these features are part of the house and are crucial for solving the problem of putting a roof over one's head. Computers and programs are the hammer, nails, and lumber of CBIS, but alone they cannot produce the information a particular organization needs. To understand information systems, one must understand the problems they are designed to solve, their architectural and design elements, and the organizational processes that lead to these solutions.

A Business Perspective on Information Systems
- From a business perspective, an information system is an organizational and management solution, based on information technology, to a challenge posed by the environment. Examine this definition closely because it emphasizes the organizational and managerial nature of information systems: To fully understand information systems, a manager must understand the broader organization, management, and information technology dimensions of systems and their power to provide solutions to challenges and problems in the business environment. We refer to this broader understanding of information systems, which encompasses an understanding of the management and organizational dimensions of systems as well as the technical dimensions of systems as information systems literacy. Information systems literacy includes a behavioral as well as a technical approach to studying information systems. Computer literacy, in contrast, focuses primarily on knowledge of information technology.

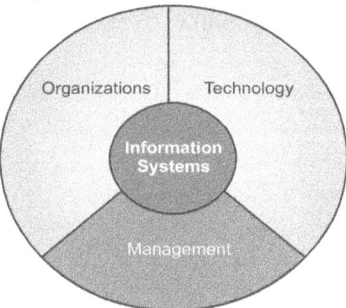

Fig. 4.4: Information systems are more than computers

- Using information systems effectively requires an understanding of the organization, management, and information technology shaping the systems. All information systems can be described as organizational and management solutions to challenges posed by the environment.
- Review the diagram at the beginning of the chapter, which reflects this expanded definition of an information system. The diagram shows how Procter & Gamble's Web site, intranet, and sales and replenishment systems solve the business challenge of being a mature business with inefficient business processes. The diagram also illustrates how management, technology, and organization elements work together to create the systems. Each chapter of this text begins with a diagram similar to this one to help you analyze the chapter opening case. You can use this diagram as a starting point for analyzing any information system or information system problem you encounter. The Manager's Toolkit provides guidelines on how to use this framework for problem solving.

Organizations
- Information systems are an integral part of organizations. Indeed, for some companies, such as credit reporting firms, without the information system there would be no business. The key elements of an organization are its people, structure, operating procedures, politics, and culture. Organizations are composed of different levels and specialties. Their structures reveal a clear-cut division of labor. Experts are employed and trained for different functions. The major business functions, or specialized tasks performed by business organizations, consist of sales and marketing, manufacturing and production, finance, accounting, and human resources

Table 4.2: Major Business Functions

Function	Purpose
Sales and marketing	Selling the organization's products and services.
Manufacturing and production	Producing products and services.
Finance	Managing the organization's financial assets (cash, stocks, bonds, etc.)
Accounting	Maintaining the organization's financial records (receipts, disbursements, paychecks, etc.); accounting for the flow of funds.
Human resources	Attracting, developing, and maintaining the organization's labor force; maintaining employee records.

- An organization coordinates work through a structured hierarchy and formal, standard operating procedures.
- The hierarchy arranges people in a pyramid structure of rising authority and responsibility. The upper levels of the hierarchy consist of managerial, professional, and technical employees, whereas the lower levels consist of operational personnel.
- Standard operating procedures (SOPs) are formal rules that have been developed over a long time for accomplishing tasks. These rules guide employees in a variety of procedures, from writing an invoice to responding to customer complaints. Most procedures are formalized and written down, but others are informal work practices, such as a requirement to return telephone calls from co-workers or customers, that are not formally documented. The firm's business processes, which we defined earlier, are based on its standard operating procedures. Many business processes and SOPs are incorporated into information systems, such as how to pay a supplier or how to correct an erroneous bill.
- Organizations require many different kinds of skills and people. In addition to managers, knowledge workers (such as engineers, architects, or scientists) design products or services and create new knowledge and data workers process the organization's paperwork. Production or service workers (such as machinists, assemblers, or packers) actually produce the organization's products or services.
- Each organization has a unique culture, or fundamental set of assumptions, values, and ways of doing things, that has been accepted by most of its members. Parts of an organization's culture can always be found embedded in its information systems. For instance, the United Parcel Service's concern with placing service to the customer first is an aspect of its organizational culture that can be found in the company's package tracking systems.
- Different levels and specialties in an organization create different interests and points of view. These views often conflict. Conflict is the basis for organizational politics. Information systems come out of this cauldron of differing perspectives, conflicts, compromises, and agreements that are a natural part of all organizations.

Management
- Managers perceive business challenges in the environment, they set the organizational strategy for responding and allocate the human and financial resources to achieve the strategy and coordinate the work.
- Throughout, they must exercise responsible leadership. Management's job is to "make sense" out of the many situations faced by organizations and formulate action plans to solve organizational problems. The business information systems described in this book reflect the hopes, dreams, and realities of real-world managers.

- But managers must do more than manage what already exists. They must also create new products and services and even re-create the organization from time to time. A substantial part of management responsibility is creative work driven by new knowledge and information. Information technology can play a powerful role in redirecting and redesigning the organization.
- It is important to note that managerial roles and decisions vary at different levels of the organization. Senior managers make long-range strategic decisions about what products and services to produce. Middle managers carry out the programs and plans of senior management. Operational managers are responsible for monitoring the firm's daily activities. All levels of management are expected to be creative, to develop novel solutions to a broad range of problems. Each level of management has different information needs and information system requirements.

Technology
- Information technology is one of many tools managers use to cope with change. Computer hardware is the physical equipment used for input, processing, and output activities in an information system. It consists of the following: the computer processing unit; various input, output, and storage devices; and physical media to link these devices together.
- Computer software consists of the detailed preprogrammed instructions that control and coordinate the computer hardware components in an information system.
- Storage technology includes both the physical media for storing data, such as magnetic or optical disk or tape, and the software governing the organization of data on these physical media.
- Communications technology, consisting of both physical devices and software, links the various pieces of hardware and transfers data from one physical location to another. Computers and communications equipment can be connected in networks for sharing voice, data, images, sound, or even video. A network links two or more computers to share data or resources such as a printer. All of these technologies represent resources that can be shared throughout the organization and constitute the firm's information technology (IT) infrastructure. The IT infrastructure provides the foundation or platform on which the firm can build its specific information systems. Each organization must carefully design and manage its information technology infrastructure so that it has the set of technology services it needs for the work it wants to accomplish with information systems. The organization element anchors the package tracking system in UPS's sales and production functions. It specifies the required procedures for identifying packages with both sender and recipient information, taking inventory, tracking the packages en

route, and providing package status reports for UPS customers and customer service representatives. The system must also provide information to satisfy the needs of managers and workers. UPS drivers need to be trained in both package pickup and delivery procedures and in how to use the package tracking system so that they can work efficiently and effectively. UPS customers may need some training to use UPS in-house package tracking software or the UPS World Wide Web site. UPS's management is responsible for monitoring service levels and costs and for promoting the company's strategy of combining low cost and superior service. Management decided to use automation to increase the ease of sending a package via UPS and of checking its delivery status, thereby reducing delivery costs and increasing sales revenues. The technology supporting this system consists of handheld computers, barcode scanners, wired and wireless communications networks, desktop computers, UPS's central computer, storage technology for the package delivery data, UPS in-house package tracking software, and software to access the World Wide Web. The result is an information system solution to the business challenge of providing a high level of service with low prices in the face of mounting competition.

Contemporary Approaches to Information Systems

- Multiple perspectives on information systems show that the study of information systems is a multidisciplinary field. No single theory or perspective dominates. Fig. 4.5 illustrates the major disciplines that contribute problems, issues, and solutions in the study of information systems. In general, the field can be divided into technical and behavioral approaches. Information systems are sociotechnical systems. Though they are composed of machines, devices, and "hard" physical technology, they require substantial social, organizational, and intellectual investments to make them work properly.

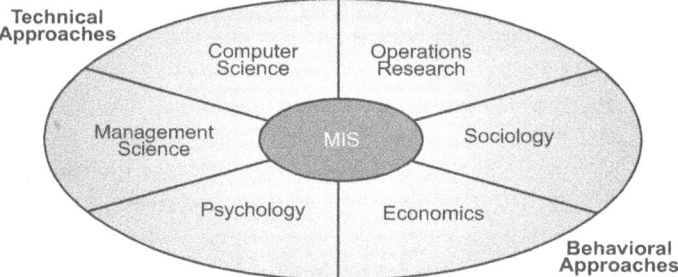

Fig. 4.5: Contemporary Approaches to Information Systems

- The study of information systems deals with issues and insights contributed from technical and behavioral disciplines.

Technical Approach
- The technical approach to information systems emphasizes mathematically based models to study information systems, as well as the physical technology and formal capabilities of these systems. The disciplines that contribute to the technical approach are computer science, management science, and operations research. Computer science is concerned with establishing theories of computability, methods of computation, and methods of efficient data storage and access. Management science emphasizes the development of models for decision-making and management practices. Operations research focuses on mathematical techniques for optimizing selected parameters of organizations, such as transportation, inventory control, and transaction costs.

4.2 Behavioral Approach

- An important part of the information systems field is concerned with behavioral issues that arise in the development and long-term maintenance of information systems. Issues such as strategic business integration, design, implementation, utilization, and management cannot be explored usefully with the models used in the technical approach. Other behavioral disciplines contribute important concepts and methods. For instance, sociologists study information systems with an eye toward how groups and organizations shape the development of systems and also how systems affect individuals, groups, and organizations. Psychologists study information systems with an interest in how human decision makers perceive and use formal information. Economists study information systems with an interest in what impact systems have on control and cost structures within the firm and within markets.

- The behavioral approach does not ignore technology. Indeed, information systems technology is often the stimulus for a behavioral problem or issue. But the focus of this approach is generally not on technical solutions. Instead it concentrates on changes in attitudes, management and organizational policy, and behavior (Kling and Dutton, 1982).

4.2.1 Approach of This Text: Sociotechnical Systems

- The study of management information systems (MIS) arose in the 1970s to focus on computer-based information systems aimed at managers (Davis and Olson, 1985). MIS combines the theoretical work of computer science, management science, and operations research with a practical orientation toward developing system solutions to real-world problems and managing information technology resources. It also pays attention to behavioral issues surrounding the development, use, and impact of information systems raised by sociology, economics, and psychology.

- Our experience as academics and practitioners leads us to believe that no single perspective effectively captures the reality of information systems. Problems with systems—and their solutions—are rarely all technical or all behavioral. Our best advice to students is to understand the perspectives of all disciplines. Indeed, the challenge and excitement of the information systems field is that it requires an appreciation and tolerance of many different approaches.

- Adopting a sociotechnical systems perspective helps to avoid a purely technological approach to information systems. For instance, the fact that information technology is rapidly declining in cost and growing in power does not necessarily or easily translate into productivity enhancement or bottom-line profits.

- In this book, we stress the need to optimize the system's performance as a whole. Both the technical and behavioral components need attention. This means that technology must be changed and designed in such a way as to fit organizational and individual needs. At times, the technology may have to be "de-optimized" to accomplish this fit. Organizations and individuals must also be changed through training, learning, and planned organizational change in order to allow the technology to operate and prosper. People and organizations change to take advantage of new information technology.

Fig. 4.6 illustrates this process of mutual adjustment in a sociotechnical system.

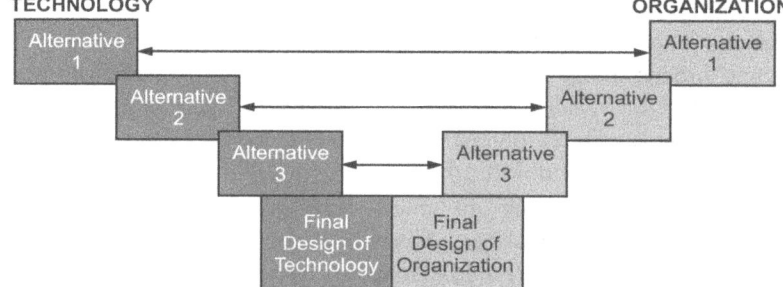

Fig. 4.6: A Sociotechnical Perspective on Information Systems

- In a sociotechnical perspective, the performance of a system is optimized when both the technology and the organization mutually adjust to one another until a satisfactory fit is obtained.

Toward the Digital Firm: The New Role of Information Systems in Organizations

- Managers cannot ignore information systems because they play such a critical role in contemporary organizations. Today's systems directly affect how managers decide, plan, and manage their employees, and, increasingly, they shape what products are produced, and where, when, and how. Therefore, responsibility for systems cannot be delegated to technical decision makers.

4.2.2 The Widening Scope of Information Systems

- Fig. 4.7 illustrates the new relationship between organizations and information systems. There is a growing interdependence between business strategy, rules, and procedures on the one hand, and information systems software, hardware, databases, and telecommunications on the other. A change in any of these components often requires changes in other components. This relationship becomes critical when management plans for the future. What a business would like to do in five years often depends on what its systems will be able to do. Increasing market share, becoming the high-quality or low-cost producer, developing new products, and increasing employee productivity depend more and more on the kinds and quality of information systems in the organization.

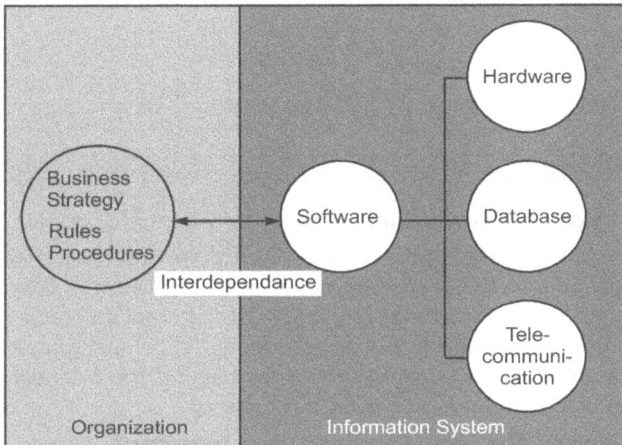

Fig. 4.7: The Interdependence between Organizations and Information Systems

- In contemporary systems there is a growing interdependence between organizational business strategy, rules, and procedures and the organization's information systems. Changes in strategy, rules, and procedures increasingly require changes in hardware, software, databases, and telecommunications. Existing systems can act as a constraint on organizations. Often, what the organization would like to do depends on what its systems will permit it to do.

- A second change in the relationship between information systems and organizations results from the growing reach and scope of system projects and applications. Building and managing systems today involves a much larger part of the organization than it did in the past. As firms become more like "digital firms," the system enterprise extends to customers, vendors, and even industry competitors Fig. 4.8. Where early systems produced largely technical changes that affected only a few people in the firm, contemporary systems have been bringing about managerial changes (who has what information about whom, when, and how often) and institutional "core" changes (what products and services are produced, under what conditions, and by whom). As companies move toward digital firm organizations, nearly all the firm's managers and employees—as well as customers and vendors—participate in a variety of firm systems, tied together by a digital information web. For instance, what a customer does on a firm's Web site can trigger an employee to make an on-the-spot pricing decision or alert a firm's suppliers of potential "stockout" situations.

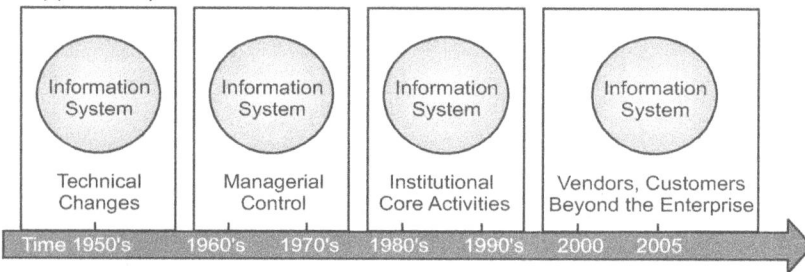

Fig. 4.8: The Widening Scope of Information Systems

- The widening scope of information systems. Over time, information systems have come to play a larger role in the life of organizations. Early systems brought about largely technical changes that were relatively easy to accomplish. Later systems affected managerial control and behavior and subsequently "core" institutional activities. In the digital firm era, information systems extend far beyond the boundaries of the firm to encompass vendors, customers, and even competitors.

4.2.3 The Network Revolution and the Internet

- One reason information systems play such a large role in organizations and affect so many people is the soaring power and declining cost of computer technology. Computing power, which has been doubling every 18 months, has improved the performance of microprocessors over 25,000 times since their invention 30 years ago. With powerful, easy-to-use software, the computer can crunch numbers, analyze vast pools of data, or simulate complex physical and logical processes with animated drawings, sounds, and even tactile feedback.

- The soaring power of computer technology has spawned powerful communication networks that organizations can use to access vast storehouses of information from around the world and to coordinate activities across space and time. These networks are transforming the shape and form of business enterprises, creating the foundation for the digital firm.

- The world's largest and most widely used network is the Internet. The Internet is an international network of networks that are both commercial and publicly owned. The Internet connects hundreds of thousands of different networks from more than 200 countries around the world. More than 500 million people working in science, education, government, and business use the Internet to exchange information or perform business transactions with other organizations around the globe.
- The Internet is extremely elastic. If networks are added or removed or failures occur in parts of the system, the rest of the Internet continues to operate. Through special communication and technology standards, any computer can communicate with virtually any other computer linked to the Internet using ordinary telephone lines. Companies and private individuals can use the Internet to exchange business transactions, text messages, graphic images, and even video and sound, whether they are located next door or on the other side of the globe.
- Fig. 4.9 describes some of the Internet's capabilities.

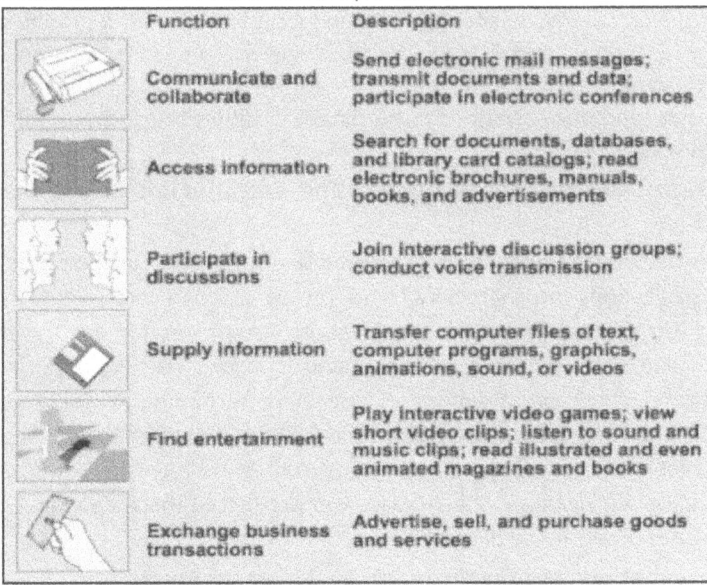

Fig. 4.9: What You Can Do on the Internet

- The Internet is creating a new "universal" technology platform on which to build all sorts of new products, services, strategies, and organizations. It is reshaping the way information systems are being used in business and daily life. By eliminating many technical, geographic, and cost barriers obstructing the global flow of information, the Internet is inspiring new uses of information systems and new business models. The Internet provides the primary technology platform for the digital firm.

- Because it offers so many new possibilities for doing business, the Internet capability known as the World Wide Web is of special interest to organizations and managers. The World Wide Web is a system with universally accepted standards for storing, retrieving, formatting, and displaying information in a networked environment. Information is stored and displayed as electronic "pages" that can contain text, graphics, animations, sound, and video. These Web pages can be linked electronically to other Web pages, regardless of where they are located, and viewed by any type of computer. By clicking on highlighted words or buttons on a Web page, you can link to related pages to find additional information, software programs, or still more links to other points on the Web. The Web can serve as the foundation for new kinds of information systems such as those based on Procter & Gamble's Web site described in the chapter opening vignette.

- All of the Web pages maintained by an organization or individual are called a Web site. Businesses are creating Web sites with stylish typography, colorful graphics, push-button interactivity, and often sound and video to disseminate product information widely, to "broadcast" advertising and messages to customers, to collect electronic orders and customer data, and, increasingly, to coordinate far-flung sales forces and organizations on a global scale.

New Options for Organizational Design: The Digital Firm and the Collaborative Enterprise

- The explosive growth in computing power and networks, including the Internet, is turning organizations into networked enterprises, allowing information to be instantly distributed within and beyond the organization. Companies can use this information to improve their internal business processes and to coordinate these business processes with those of other organizations. These new technologies for connectivity and collaboration can be used to redesign and reshape organizations, transforming their structure, scope of operations, reporting and control mechanisms, work practices, work flows, products, and services. The ultimate end product of these new ways of conducting business electronically is the digital firm.

Flattening Organizations and the Changing Management Process

- Large, bureaucratic organizations, which primarily developed before the computer age, are often inefficient, slow to change, and less competitive than newly created organizations. Some of these large organizations have downsized, reducing the number of employees and the number of levels in their organizational hierarchies. For example, when Eastman Chemical Co. split off from Kodak in 1994 it had $3.3 billion in revenue and 24,000 full-time employees. By 2000 it generated $5 billion in revenue with only 17,000 employees.

- In digital firms, hierarchy and organizational levels do not disappear. But digital firms develop "optimal hierarchies" that balance the decision-making load across an organization, resulting in flatter organizations. Flatter organizations have fewer levels of management, with lower-level employees being given greater decision-making authority Fig. 4.10. Those employees are empowered to make more decisions than in the past, they no longer work standard nine-to-five hours, and they no longer necessarily work in an office. Moreover, such employees may be scattered geographically, sometimes working half a world away from the manager.

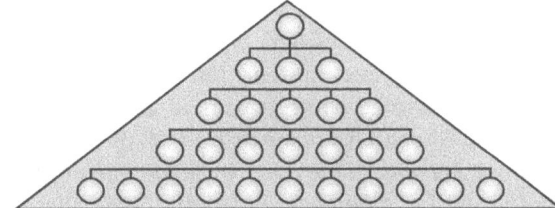

A traditional hierarchical organisation with many levels of management

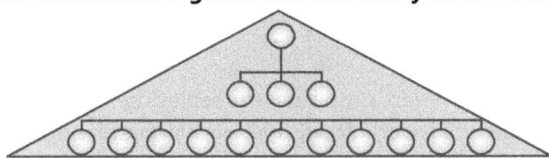

A organisation that has been 'flattened' by removing layers of management

Fig. 4.10: Flattening Organizations

- Information systems can reduce the number of levels in an organization by providing managers with information to supervise larger numbers of workers and by giving lowerlevel employees more decision-making authority. These changes mean that the management span of control has also been broadened, allowing high-level managers to manage and control more workers spread over greater distances. Many companies have eliminated thousands of middle managers as a result of these changes. AT&T, IBM, and General Motors are only a few of the organizations that have eliminated more than 30,000 middle managers in one fell swoop.

- Information technology is also recasting the management process by providing powerful new tools for more precise planning, forecasting, and monitoring. For instance, it is now possible for managers to obtain information on organizational performance down to the level of specific transactions from just about anywhere in the organization at any time. Product managers at Frito-Lay Corporation, the world's largest manufacturer of salty snack foods, can know within hours precisely how many bags of Fritos have sold on any street in America at its customers' stores, how much they sold for, and what the competition's sales volumes and prices are.

Separating Work from Location

- Communications technology has eliminated distance as a factor for many types of work in many situations. Salespersons can spend more time in the field with customers and have more up-to-date information with them while carrying much less paper. Many employees can work remotely from their homes or cars, and companies can reserve space at smaller central offices for meeting clients or other employees. Collaborative teamwork across thousands of miles has become a reality as designers work on a new product together even if they are located on different continents. Lockheed Martin Aeronautics developed a real-time system for collaborative product design and engineering based on the Internet, which it uses to coordinate tasks with its partners such as BAE and Northrup Grumman. Engineers from all three companies work jointly on designs over the Internet. Previously, the company and its partners worked separately on designs, hammering out design differences in lengthy face-to-face meetings. A drawing that once took 400 hours now takes 125 and the design phase of projects has been cut in half.

Reorganizing Work Flows

- Information systems have been progressively replacing manual work procedures with automated work procedures, work flows, and work processes. Electronic work flows have reduced the cost of operations in many companies by displacing paper and the manual routines that accompany it. Improved work flow management has enabled many corporations not only to cut costs significantly but also to improve customer service at the same time. For instance, insurance companies can reduce processing of applications for new insurance from weeks to days Fig. 4.11.

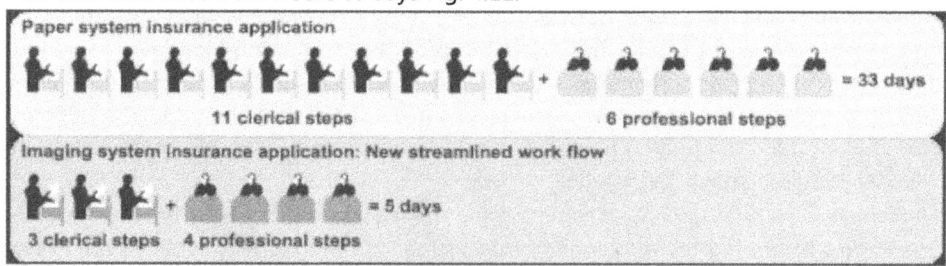

Fig. 4.11: Redesigned Work Flow for Insurance Underwriting

- An application requiring 33 days in a paper system would only take five days using computers, networks, and a streamlined work flow. Redesigned work flows can have a profound impact on organizational efficiency and can even lead to new organizational structures, products, and services.

Increasing Flexibility of Organizations

- Companies can use communications technology to organize in more flexible ways, increasing their ability to sense and respond to changes in the marketplace and to take advantage of new opportunities. Information systems can give both large and small organizations additional flexibility to overcome some of the limitations posed by their size. Table 4.3 describes some of the ways in which information technology can help small companies act "big" and help big companies act "small." Small organizations can use information systems to acquire some of the muscle and reach of larger organizations. They can perform coordinating activities, such as processing bids or keeping track of inventory, and many manufacturing tasks with very few managers, clerks, or production workers.

Table 4.3: How Information Technology Increases Organizational Flexibility

Small Companies
Desktop machines, inexpensive computer-aided design (CAD) software, and computer controlled machine tools provide the precision, speed, and quality of giant manufacturers.
Information immediately accessed by telephone and communications links eliminates the need for research staff and business libraries.
Managers can easily obtain the information they need to manage large numbers of employees in widely scattered locations.

Large Companies
Custom manufacturing systems allow large factories to offer customized products in small quantities.
Massive databases of customer purchasing records can be analyzed so that large companies know their customers' needs and preferences as easily as local merchants.
Information can be easily distributed down the ranks of the organization to empower lower-level employees and work groups to solve problems.

- Large organizations can use information technology to achieve some of the agility and responsiveness of small organizations. One aspect of this phenomenon is mass customization, the ability to offer individually tailored products or services on a large scale. Information systems can make the production process more flexible so that products can be tailored to each customer's unique set of requirements. Software and computer networks can be used to link the plant floor tightly with orders, design, and purchasing and to finely control production machines so that products can be turned out in greater variety and easily customized with no added cost for small production runs. For example, Levi Strauss has equipped its stores with an option called Original Spin, which allows customers to design jeans to their own specifications, rather than picking the jeans off the rack. Customers enter their measurements into a personal computer, which then transmits the customer's specifications over a network to Levi's plants. The company is able to produce the custom jeans on the same lines that manufacture its standard items. There are almost no extra production costs because the process does not require additional warehousing, production overruns, and inventories. Lands' End has implemented a similar system for customizing chino slacks that allows customers to enter their measurements over its Web site.

- A related trend is micromarketing, in which information systems can help companies pinpoint tiny target markets for these finely customized products and services—as small as individualized "markets of one."

Redefining Organizational Boundaries: New Avenues for Collaboration

- A key feature of the emerging digital firm is the ability to conduct business across firm boundaries almost as efficiently and effectively as it can conduct business within the firm. Networked information systems allow companies to coordinate with other organizations across great distances. Transactions such as payments and purchase orders can be exchanged electronically among different companies, thereby reducing the cost of obtaining products and services from outside the firm. Organizations can also share business data, catalogs, or mail messages through networks. These networked information systems can create new efficiencies and new relationships between an organization, its customers, and suppliers, redefining organizational boundaries.

- For example, the Toyota Motor Corporation is networked to suppliers, such as the Dana Corporation of Toledo, Ohio, a tier-one supplier of chassis, engines, and other major automotive components. Through this electronic link, the Dana Corporation monitors Toyota production and ships components exactly when needed. Toyota and Dana have thus become linked business partners with mutually shared responsibilities.

- The information system linking Toyota to its supplier is called an interorganizational information system. Systems linking a company to its customers, distributors, or suppliers are termed interorganizational systems because they automate the flow of information across organizational boundaries. Digital firms use interorganizational systems to link with suppliers, customers, and sometimes even competitors, to create and distribute new products and services without being limited by traditional organizational boundaries or physical locations. For example, Cisco Systems, described in the chapter ending case study, does not manufacture the networking products it sells; it uses other companies, such as Flextronics, for this purpose.

- Cisco uses the Internet to transmit orders to Flextronics and to monitor the status of orders as they are being shipped.
- Many of these interorganizational systems are becoming increasingly based on Web technology and providing more intense sharing of knowledge, resources, and business processes than in the past. Firms are using these systems to work jointly with suppliers and other business partners on product design and development and on the scheduling and flow of work in manufacturing, procurement, and distribution. These new levels of interfirm collaboration and coordination can lead to higher levels of efficiency, value to customers, and ultimately significant competitive advantage.

The Digital Firm: Electronic Commerce, Electronic Business, and New Digital Relationships

- The changes we have just described represent new ways of conducting business electronically both inside and outside the firm that can ultimately result in the creation of digital firms. Increasingly, the Internet is providing the underlying technology for these changes. The Internet can link thousands of organizations into a single network, creating the foundation for a vast electronic marketplace. An electronic market is an information system that links together many buyers and sellers to exchange information, products, services, and payments. Through computers and networks, these systems function like electronic intermediaries, with lowered costs for typical marketplace transactions, such as matching buyers and sellers, establishing prices, ordering goods, and paying bills (Bakos, 1998). Buyers and sellers can complete purchase and sale transactions digitally, regardless of their location.
- A vast array of goods and services are being advertised, bought, and exchanged worldwide using the Internet as a global marketplace. Companies are furiously creating eye-catching electronic brochures, advertisements, product manuals, and order forms on the World Wide Web. All kinds of products and services are available on the Web, including fresh flowers, books, real estate, musical recordings, electronics, and steaks. Even electronic financial trading has arrived on the Web for stocks, bonds, mutual funds, and other financial instruments.

- Increasingly the Web is being used for business-to-business transactions as well. For example, airlines can use the Boeing Corporation's Web site to order parts electronically and check the status of their orders. Altranet Energy Technologies of Houston operates an on-line marketplace called altranet.com where many different energy industry suppliers and buyers can meet any time of day or night to trade natural gas, liquids, electricity, and crude oil in a spot market for immediate delivery. Participants can select their trading partners, confirm transactions, and obtain credit and insurance.
- The global availability of the Internet for the exchange of transactions between buyers and sellers has fuelled the growth of electronic commerce. Electronic commerce is the process of buying and selling goods and services electronically with computerized business transactions using the Internet, networks, and other digital technologies. It also encompasses activities supporting those market transactions, such as advertising, marketing, customer support, delivery, and payment. By replacing manual and paper-based procedures with electronic alternatives, and by using information flows in new and dynamic ways, electronic commerce can accelerate ordering, delivery, and payment for goods and services while reducing companies' operating and inventory costs.
- The Internet has emerged as the primary technology platform for electronic commerce. Equally important,
- Internet technology is facilitating management of the rest of the business—publishing employee personnel policies, reviewing account balances and production plans, scheduling plant repairs and maintenance, and revising design documents. Companies are taking advantage of the connectivity and ease of use of Internet technology to create internal corporate networks called intranets that are based on Internet technology. The chapter opening vignette described how Procter & Gamble set up a private intranet for employees to publish reports, charts, and their ideas for improving the company. The number of these private intranets for organizational communication, collaboration, and coordination is soaring. In this text, we use the term electronic business to distinguish these uses of Internet and digital technology for the management and coordination of other business processes from electronic commerce.
- The Window on Organizations showed how Li & Fung allowed its suppliers and business partners to access portions of its private intranet. Private intranets extended to authorized users outside the organization are called extranets, and firms use such networks to coordinate their activities with other firms for electronic commerce and electronic business. Table 4.5 lists some examples of electronic commerce and electronic business.

Table 4.5: Examples of Electronic Commerce and Electronic Business

Electronic Commerce
Drugstore.com operates a virtual pharmacy on the Internet selling prescription medicine and over-the-counter health, beauty, and wellness products. Customers can input their orders via Drugstore.com's Web site and have their purchases shipped to them.
Travelocity provides a Web site that can be used by consumers for travel and vacation planning. Visitors can find out information on airlines, hotels, vacation packages, and other travel and leisure topics, and they can make airline and hotel reservations on-line through the Web site.
Milwaukee Electric Tool, a subsidiary of the Atlas Copco AB global industrial machine tools conglomerate based in Stockholm, created a secure sales extranet that allows its distributors to search the company's product catalog and order equipment.
Electronic Business
Roche Bioscience scientists worldwide use an intranet to share research results and discuss findings. The intranet also provides a company telephone directory and newsletter.
Texas Instruments uses an intranet to provide employees with a consolidated report of all of their compensation and benefits, including pension plans, 401K employee savings plans, and stock purchase plans. Employees can use charts and modeling tools to see the value of their portfolios and benefits now and in the future.
Dream Works SKG uses an intranet to check the daily status of projects, including animation objects, and to coordinate movie scenes.

- Fig. 4.12 illustrates a digital firm making intensive use of Internet and digital technology for electronic commerce and electronic business. Information can flow seamlessly among different parts of the company and between the company and external entities—its customers, suppliers, and business partners. Organizations will move toward this digital firm vision as they use the Internet, intranets, and extranets to manage their internal processes and their relationships with customers, suppliers, and other external entities..

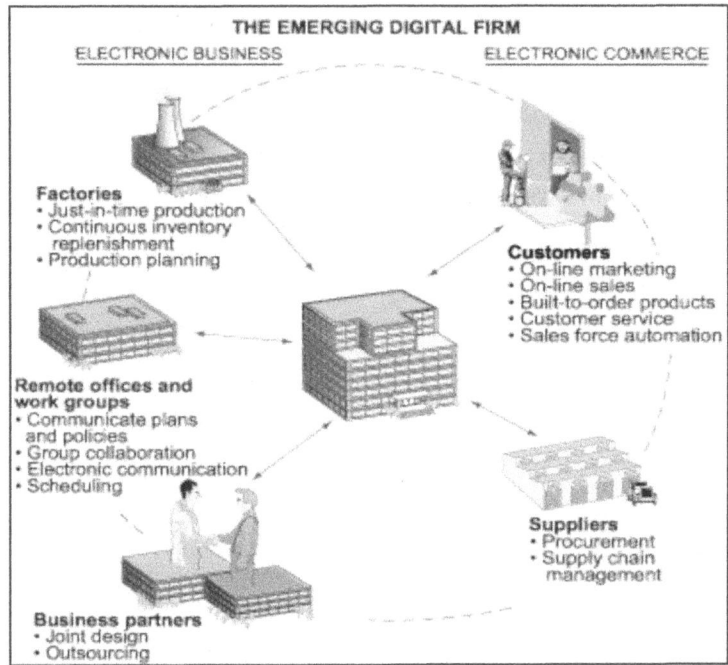

Fig. 4.12: Electronic Commerce and Electronic Business In the Emerging Digital Firm

- Electronic commerce uses Internet and digital technology to conduct transactions with customers and suppliers, whereas electronic business uses these technologies for the management of the rest of the business.
- Both electronic commerce and electronic business can fundamentally change the way business is conducted. To use the Internet and other digital technologies successfully for electronic commerce, electronic business, and the creation of digital firms, organizations may have to redefine their business models, reinvent business processes, change corporate cultures, and create much closer relationships with customers and suppliers. We discuss these issues in greater detail in following chapters.

4.3 Learning to Use Information Systems: New Opportunities with Technology

- Although information systems are creating many exciting opportunities for both businesses and individuals, they are also a source of new problems, issues, and challenges for managers. In this course, you will learn about both the challenges and opportunities information systems present, and you will be able to use information technology to enrich your learning experience.

The Challenge of Information Systems: Key Management Issues

- Although information technology is advancing at a blinding pace, there is nothing easy or mechanical about building and using information systems. There are five key challenges confronting managers:
    1. **The Strategic Business Challenge: Realizing the Digital Firm:** How can businesses use information technology to become competitive, effective, and digitally enabled? Creating a digital firm and obtaining benefits is a long and difficult journey for most organizations. Despite heavy information technology investments, many organizations are not obtaining significant business benefits, nor are they becoming digitally enabled. The power of computer hardware and software has grown much more rapidly than the ability of organizations to apply and use this technology. To fully benefit from information technology, realize genuine productivity, and take advantage of digital firm capabilities, many organizations actually need to be redesigned. They will have to make fundamental changes in organizational behavior, develop new business models, and eliminate the inefficiencies of outmoded organizational structures. If organizations merely automate what they are doing today, they are largely missing the potential of information technology.
    2. **The Globalization Challenge:** How can firms understand the business and system requirements of a global economic environment? The rapid growth in international trade and the emergence of a global economy call for information systems that can support both producing and selling goods in many different countries. In the past, each regional office of a multinational corporation focused on solving its own unique information problems. Given language, cultural, and political differences among countries, this focus frequently resulted in chaos and the failure of central management controls. To develop integrated, multinational, information systems, businesses must develop global hardware, software, and communications standards; create cross-cultural accounting and reporting structures and design transnational business processes.
    3. **The Information Architecture and Infrastructure Challenge:** How can organizations develop an information architecture and information technology infrastructure that can support their goals when business conditions and technologies are changing so rapidly? Meeting the business and technology challenges of today's digital economy requires redesigning the organization and building a new information architecture and information technology (IT) infrastructure. Information architecture is the particular form that information technology takes in an organization to achieve selected goals or functions. It is a design for the business application systems that serve each functional specialty and level of the organization and the specific ways that they are used by each organization. As firms move toward digital firm organizations and technologies, information architectures are increasingly being designed around business processes

and clusters of system applications spanning multiple functions and organizational levels. Because managers and employees directly interact with these systems, it is critical for organizational success that the information architecture meet business requirements now and in the future. Figure 1-12 illustrates the major elements of information architecture that managers will need to develop now and in the future. The architecture shows the firm's business application systems for each of the major functional areas of the organization, including sales and marketing, manufacturing, finance, accounting, and human resources. It also shows application systems supporting business processes spanning multiple organizational levels and functions within the enterprise and extending outside the enterprise to systems of suppliers, distributors, business partners, and customers. The firm's IT infrastructure provides the technology platform for this architecture. Computer hardware, software, data and storage technology, networks, and human resources required to operate the equipment constitute the shared IT resources of the firm and are available to all of its applications. Contemporary IT infrastructures are linked to public infrastructures such as the Internet. Although this technology platform is typically operated by technical personnel, general management must decide how to allocate the resources it has assigned to hardware, software, data storage, and telecommunications networks to make sound information technology investments.

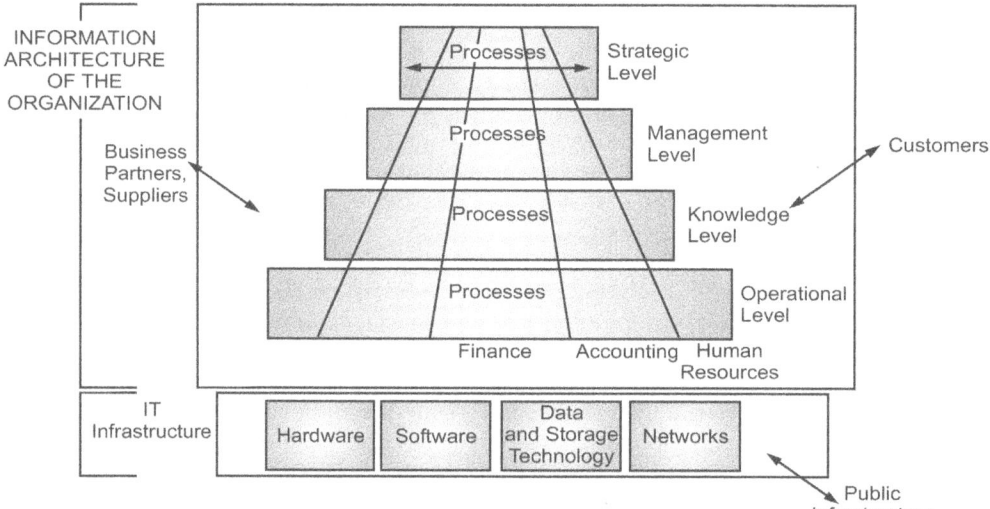

Fig. 4.13: Information Architecture and Information Technology Infrastructure

Today's managers must know how to arrange and coordinate the various computer technologies and business system applications to meet the information needs of each level of the organization, and the needs of the organization as a whole. Typical questions regarding information architecture and IT infrastructure facing today's managers include the following: Should the corporate sales data and function be distributed to each corporate remote site, or should they be centralized at headquarters? Should the organization build systems to connect the entire enterprise or separate islands of applications? Should the organization extend its infrastructure outside its boundaries to link to customers or suppliers? There is no one right answer to each of these questions. Moreover, business needs are constantly changing, which requires the IT architecture to be reassessed continually.

Creating the information architecture and IT infrastructure for a digital firm is an especially formidable task. Most companies are crippled by fragmented and incompatible computer hardware, software, telecommunications networks, and information systems that prevent information from flowing freely between different parts of the organization. Although Internet standards are solving some of these connectivity problems, creating data and computing platforms that span the enterprise—and, increasingly, link the enterprise to external business partners—is rarely as seamless as promised. Many organizations are still struggling to integrate their islands of information and technology into a coherent architecture.

4. **The Information Systems Investment Challenge:** How can organizations determine the business value of information systems? A major problem raised by the development of powerful, inexpensive computers involves not technology but management and organizations. It's one thing to use information technology to design, produce, deliver, and maintain new products. It's another thing to make money doing it. How can organizations obtain a sizable payoff from their investment in information systems?

   Engineering massive organizational and system changes in the hope of positioning a firm strategically is complicated and expensive. Senior management can be expected to ask these questions: Are we receiving the kind of return on investment from our systems that we should be? Do our competitors get more? Understanding the costs and benefits of building a single system is difficult enough; it is daunting to consider whether the entire systems effort is "worth it." Imagine, then, how a senior executive must think when presented with a major transformation in information architecture and IT infrastructure—a bold venture in organizational change costing tens of millions of dollars and taking many years.

5. **The Responsibility and Control Challenge:** How can organizations ensure that their information systems are used in an ethically and socially responsible manner? How can we design information systems that people can control and understand?

Although information systems have provided enormous benefits and efficiencies, they have also created new problems and challenges of which managers should be aware. Table 4.6 describes some of these problems and challenges.

Table 4.6 Positive and Negative Impacts of Information Systems

Benefit of Information Systems	Negative Impact
• Information systems can perform calculations or process paperwork much faster than people.	• By automating activities that were previously performed by people, information systems may eliminate jobs.
• Information systems can help companies learn more about the purchase patterns and preferences of their customers.	• Information systems may allow organizations to collect personal details about people that violate their privacy.
• Information systems provide new efficiencies through services such as automated teller machines (ATMs), telephone systems, or computer-controlled airplanes and air terminals.	• Information systems are used in so many aspects of everyday life that system outages can cause shutdowns of businesses or transportation services, paralyzing communities.
• Information systems have made possible new medical advances in surgery, radiology, and patient monitoring.	• Heavy users of information systems may suffer repetitive stress injury, technostress, and other health problems.
• The Internet distributes information instantly to millions of people across the world.	• The Internet can be used to distribute illegal copies of software, books, articles, and other intellectual property.

- A major management challenge is making informed decisions that are sensitive to the negative consequences of information systems as well to the positive ones.
- Managers will also be faced with ongoing problems of security and control. Information systems are so essential to business, government, and daily life that organizations must take special steps to ensure that they are accurate, reliable, and secure. A firm invites disaster if it uses systems that don't work as intended, that don't deliver information in a form that people can interpret correctly and use, or that have control rooms where controls don't work or where instruments give false signals. Information systems must be designed so that they function as intended and so that humans can control the process.
- Managers will need to ask: Can we apply high quality assurance standards to our information systems, as well as to our products and services? Can we build information

systems that respect people's rights of privacy while still pursuing our organization's goals? Should information systems monitor employees? What do we do when an information system designed to increase efficiency and productivity eliminates people's jobs?

4.4 Overview of World Wide Web (Web Server and Client)

- The term WWW refers to the World Wide Web or simply the Web.
- The World Wide Web consists of all the public websites connected to the internet worldwide, including the client devices (such as computers and cell phones) that access web content.
- The WWW is just one of many applications of the internet and computer networks.
- The World Wide Web is a system of interlinked hypertext documents accessed via the internet. With a web browser, one can view web pages that may contain text, images, videos, and other multimedia, and navigate between them via hyperlinks.
- The World Wide Web is based on technologies like HTML (Hypertext Markup Language), HTTP (Hypertext Transfer Protocol) and Web servers and Web browsers.

4.4.1 Definition

- The World Wide Web Consortium (W3C) define WWW as "The World Wide Web is the universe of network-accessible information, an embodiment of human knowledge."

OR

- "An internet-wide distributed hypermedia information retrieval system which provides access to a large universe of documents"

OR

- A technical definition of the World Wide Web is "all the resources and users on the internet that are using the Hypertext Transfer Protocol (HTTP)".

1. **Web Server:**
- A server is a computer program that provides services to other computer programs (and their users) in the same or other computers.
- A Web Server is a Computer or Combination of computers, which is connected through internet or intranet to serve the clients quests, coming from their web browser.
- It is a large repository of web pages which transfer to the client in response to their request. The client request to the server through protocol such as FTP, HTTP, SMTP etc for their own specific use.
- Every web server has a unique IP address and domain name which identifies that machine on the network.
- A server contains the server software installed on it, which manages the client request and response them.

Fig. 4.14: Web server

- Web server interacts with the client through a web browser. It delivers the web pages to the client and to an application by using the web browser and the HTTP protocols respectively.
- We can also define the web server as the package of large number of programs installed on a computer connected to internet or intranet for downloading the requested files using File Transfer Protocol, serving e-mail and building and publishing web pages.
- There are many types of web server, Enterprise uses according to their need. Some of the popular category of web servers are:
   (i) **HTTP Server:** It handles HTTP request coming from clients browser and transfer the static pages to client in response to their request. This pages runs of the client browser. It generally contains the static pages.
   (ii) **Application Server:** It is installed database and web servers.
   (iii) **FTP Server:** This type of server is used for file transfer from one machine (Computer) to another using the internet or intranet. It uses File Transfer Protocols to transfer file from one computer to another. Such type of server uses some file transfer policies, authentication, login validation etc.
   (iv) **Apache Tomcat** is popular web server being used today for the implementation of some java technologies. It is a open source software used for implementing web applications.
   (v) **Mail Server:** A Mail Server store and retrieve mail messages from client mail box.

2. **Clients:**
- Independent computers connected to a server are called clients.
- A client is the requesting program or user in a client/server relationship.
- For example, the user of a Web browser is effectively making client requests for pages from servers all over the Web.
- The browser itself is a client in its relationship with the computer that is getting and returning the requested HTML file. The computer handling the request and sending back the HTML file is a server.

4.4.2 How does the WWW Work?
- World Wide Web works on the client-server model.
- A user computer works as a client which can receive and send data to the server.
- When a web page is requested by a user, the browser contacts the requested server (where the website is stored) and by fetching and interpreting the requested files, it displays the web page on the computer screen.

- Information is stored in documents called web pages and the web pages are files stored on computers called Web servers.
- Computers reading the web pages and these web clients view the pages with a program called a web browser.

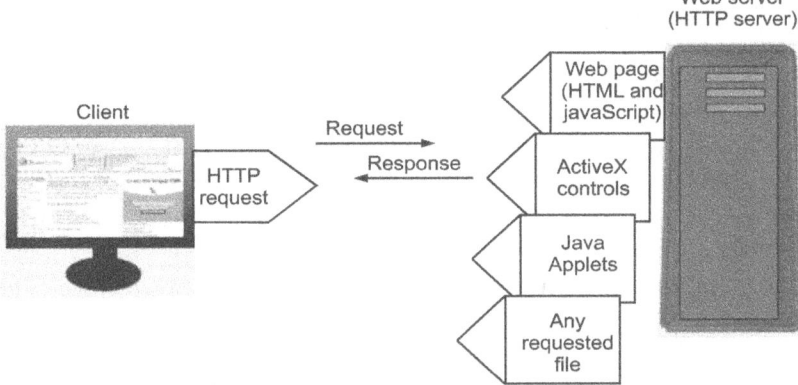

Fig. 4.15: Working of server and client (www client-server model)

4.5 Management Issues and Decisions

- Enterprises have made significant investment s in network and systems management solutions and processes. The focus of IT is shifting from merely gathering massive amounts of data to targeting and delivering information to people who can act on it in a timely fashion, no matter where they are. If we think of the evolution on computing machines from ENIAC-1946 to today's mobile phone and software from first proposed by Alan Turing in his 1935 essay Computable numbers with an application to the Decision problem to the today's systems and programming software the management of hardware and software have improved and become complex.

1. **Mintzberg's managerial role models**
- Mintzberg identified ten separate roles in managerial work, each role defined as an organized collection of behaviors belonging to an identifiable function or position. He separated these roles into three subcategories: interpersonal contact (1, 2, 3), information processing (4, 5, 6) and decision making (7-10).
    1. Figurehead: the manager performs ceremonial and symbolic duties as head of the organization
    2. Leader: fosters a proper work atmosphere and motivates and develops subordinates
    3. Liaison: develops and maintains a network of external contacts to gather information

4. Monitor: gathers internal and external information relevant to the organization
5. Disseminator: transmits factual and value based information to subordinates
6. Spokesperson: communicates to the outside world on performance and policies
7. Entrepreneur: designs and initiates change in the organization
8. Disturbance handler: deals with unexpected events and operational breakdowns
9. Resource allocator: controls and authorizes the use of organizational resources
10. Negotiator: participates in negotiation activities with other organizations and individuals Mintzberg next analyzed individual manager's use and mix of the ten roles according to the six work related characteristics. He identified four clusters of independent variables: external, function related, individual and situational. He concluded that eight role combinations were 'natural' configurations of the job:
    - Contact manager -- figurehead and liaison
    - Political manager -- spokesperson and negotiator
    - Entrepreneur -- entrepreneur and negotiator
    - Insider -- resource allocator
    - Real-time manager -- disturbance handler
    - Team manager -- leader
    - Expert manager -- monitor and spokesperson
    - New manager -- liaison and monitor

Today, this study which is made at 1973 still valid, maybe we may add keep track of legislation and laws.

2. Managements issues in IT Management

- With the evolution of computing machines managements in IT Management improved and increased. At Eniac time, in 1946 there were programmers like Jean Bartik, Electrical Engineers like Dr. John Vincent Atanasoff and academicians like Dr. John W. Mauchly and Dr. J. Presper Eckert. There were no need for management; they were trying to find faster ways to perform mathematical computations. UNIVAC I was the first mass-produced computer. In 1956, Westinghouse Electric Company installed a UNIVAC computer in its East Pittsburgh plant. The UNIVAC was used to calculate company payrolls, sales records, analysis of sales performance and other company business. Management practice began at this point.
- There was a need for programmers and operators which were operating the system and preparing magnetic tapes. Therefore the managements below were required.
    1. Service Management
    2. Development Management

3. Human Management
4. Systems Management
5. Time Management
6. Performance Management
7. Data Management
8. Stress Management
9. Problem Management
10. Scientific Management
11. Release Management
12. Business Process Management
13. Project Management
14. Change Management
15. Strategic Management
16. Network Management
17. Helpdesk Management
18. Application Management
19. Knowledge Management
20. Investment Management
21. Configuration Management
22. Rights Management
23. Life cycle Management
24. IT Financial Management
25. Security Management
26. Content Management
27. Risk Management
28. Lean Management
29. Resource Management
30. Incident Management
31. Alert Management
32. Capacity Management
33. Patch Management
34. Role Management
35. Relationship Management

36. Portfolio Management
37. Regulation Management
38. Outsourcing Management
39. Asset Management
40. Archive Management

- Now, let's take a close look at that forty management issues in IT Management.

1. **Service Management**

    Service management is generally concerned with the "back office" or operational concerns of information technology management. The concept of "service" in an IT sense has a distinct operational connotation, but it would be incorrect then to assume that IT Service Management is only about IT operations.

    Service management is usually used in conjunction with operations support systems. Systems that use service management can include order management, inventory management, activation, maintenance, performance diagnostics and several other types of support systems to make sure that these systems are running proficiently and error free. IT Service Management overlaps with the disciplines of business service management and Problem Management, Incident Management, Capacity Management, Network Management, Helpdesk Management, IT portfolio management, especially in the area of IT planning and financial control.

2. **Development Management**

    Software development is about working to produce/create software. The term software development is often used for the activity of computer programming, which is the process of writing and maintaining the source code. Software development may include research, new development, modification, reuse, re-engineering, maintenance, or any other activities that result in software products. For larger software systems, usually developed by a team of people, some form of process is typically followed to guide the stages of production of the software.

3. **Human Management**

    Finding the right employees at the right times can be an especially time-consuming and frustrating struggle. Recruitment strategies for hiring employees should be set with Human Resources Manager. IT managers should also consider employee coaching, coaching for performance and they must know how to deal with difficult employees. Like any other manager, IT Manager must track employee time for costing and of course for the health of the projects in hand.

4. **Systems Management**

   Systems management is the general area of IT that concerns installing, configuring, administering and managing computer resources, especially network resources. System management may involve one or more of the following tasks:
   - Hardware inventories.
   - Server availability monitoring and metrics.
   - Software inventory and installation, configuration and maintain.
   - Anti-virus and anti-malware management.
   - User's activities monitoring.
   - Capacity monitoring.
   - Security management.
   - Storage management.
   - Network capacity and utilization monitoring.

5. **Time Management**

   Time management is the art of arranging, organizing, scheduling, and budgeting one's time for the purpose of generating more effective work and productivity.

   The Management Process:
   - Plan—specify what goals you want to achieve. Visualize the end results. Break large goals into weekly and daily priorities and detail the steps to completion. Be prepared for barriers and deal with them in a calm manner.
   - Organize—your activities to achieve your goals. Use project boards, be ready for busy weeks, and organize your work space.
   - Staff—ask for help, delegate tasks, form study groups, take advantage of supportive programs.
   - Direct—use positive reinforcement to motivate yourself. Reward yourself.
   - Evaluate—Monitor your attitude and behavior. Track your accomplishments.

6. **Performance Management**
   - Performance management includes activities to ensure that goals are consistently being met in an effective and efficient manner.
   - IT Performance management is refers to the monitoring and measurement of relevant metrics to assess the performance of IT resources. It can be used in both a business context (IT Management), and an IT Operations context. In a business context, IT Performance Management is concerned with measuring the expenditure of capital and human resources in IT projects to determine how they improve strategic and operational capabilities of the firm in designing and developing

products and services for maximum customer satisfaction, corporate productivity, profitability and competitiveness. In an operations context, IT Performance Management is the subset of tools and processes in IT Operations which deals with the collection, monitoring and analysis of metrics that can tell IT staff if a system component is up and running, or if the metrics indicate abnormal behavior that can impact the components' ability to function correctly - much like how a doctor may measure pulse, respiration, and temperature to measure how the human body is "operating".

7. **Data Management**
    o Data management is the process of developing data architectures, practices and procedures dealing with data and then executing these aspects on a regular basis. It is; controlling, protecting, and facilitating access to data in order to provide information consumers with timely access to the data they need.
    o There are many topics within data management, some of the more popular topics include data modeling, data warehousing, data movement, database administration and data mining

8. **Stress Management**
    o Managing stress is all about taking charge: taking charge of your thoughts, your emotions, your schedule, your environment, and the way you deal with problems. The ultimate goal is a balanced life, with time for work, relationships, relaxation, and fun – plus the resilience to hold up under pressure and meet challenges head on.
    o Stress management has strong relation with time management and task management. Correctly balanced schedule, prioritized tasks and delegation reduce the stress.

9. **Problem Management**
    o The goal of Problem Management is to minimize the adverse impact of Incidents and Problems on the business that is caused by errors within the IT Infrastructure, and to prevent recurrence of Incidents related to these errors. In order to achieve this goal, Problem Management seeks to get to the root cause of Incidents and then initiate actions to improve or correct the situation

10. **Scientific Management**
    o In the mid-nineteenth century, traditional management practices were found to be inadequate to meet demands from the changing economic, social and technological environment. Numerous enterprises were simply functioning inefficiently. A few pioneers examined the causes of these inefficiencies and tried to try to find more efficient methods and procedures for running a firm. These basic experiments gave

birth to a system which became known as scientific management. Its method relied heavily on finding the "one best way" to solve every operating using scientific methods of research. The concept involved a way of thinking about management.
- F.W. Taylor, in 1911, published his most famous book: principles of scientific management He was among the first experts who systematically tried to formulate some universal management principles:
  - Workers should have a detailed, clearly defined, daily task;
  - Standardized conditions are needed to ensure the task is more easily accomplished;
  - High payment should be given to the workers who managed to successfully complete their tasks. Workers who failed to their standards, in turn, should be sanctioned and receive less compensation.

11. Release Management
- Release Management is the relatively new but rapidly growing discipline within software engineering of managing software releases.
- A Release Manager is:
  - Facilitator – serves as a liaison between varying business units to guarantee smooth and timely delivery of software products or updates.
  - Gatekeeper – "holds the keys" to production systems/applications and takes responsibility for their implementations.
  - Architect – helps to identify, create and/or implement processes or products to efficiently manage the release of code.
  - Server Application Support Engineer – help troubleshoot problems with an application (although not typically at a code level).
  - Coordinator – utilized to coordinate disparate source trees, projects, teams and components.
  - Some of the challenges facing a Software Release Manager include the management of:
  - Software Defects
  - Issues
  - Risks
  - Software Change Requests
  - New Development Requests (additional features and functions)
  - Deployment and Packaging
  - New Development Tasks

12. Business Process Management
- First let's define the core element, a business process. A business process is an aggregation of operations performed by people and software systems containing the information used in the process, along with the applicable business rules. The execution of a business process achieves a business objective. Processes also include business rules that may be documented policies and procedures, as well as the undocumented 'how we really do things' rules that exist in most enterprises.
- A comprehensive Business Process Management platform provides an organization with the ability to collectively define their business processes, deploy those processes as applications accessible via integrated existing software systems, and then provide managers with the visibility to monitor, analyze, control and improve the execution of those processes in real time.

13. Project Management
- Project is the collection of activities that are related or connected, for developing a product or a service. It is a temporary effort to create a unique product or service. Project management is a methodical approach to planning and guiding project processes from start to finish. The processes are guided through five stages: initiation, planning, executing, controlling, and closing.
- The scope of project management knowledge as follows: integration, scope, time, cost, quality, human resources, communications, risk, and procurement. So, Project management has cross relations with other managements' issues in IT.

14. Change Management
- Change Management is an IT Service Management discipline. The objective of Change Management in this context is to ensure that standardized methods and procedures are used for efficient and prompt handling of all changes to controlled IT infrastructure, in order to minimize the number and impact of any related incidents upon service. Changes in the IT infrastructure may arise reactively in response to problems or externally imposed requirements, e.g. legislative changes, or proactively from seeking improved efficiency and effectiveness or to enable or reflect business initiatives, or from programs, projects or service improvement initiatives. Change Management can ensure standardized methods, processes and procedures are used for all changes, facilitate efficient and prompt handling of all changes, and maintain the proper balance between the need for change and the potential detrimental impact of changes.
- Change management is responsible for managing change process involving:
    - Hardware
    - Communications equipment and software
    - System software
    - All documentation and procedures associated with the running, support and maintenance of live systems

15. Strategic Management
- It is the art of planning your business at the highest possible level. Strategic management focuses on building a solid underlying structure to your business that will subsequently be fleshed out through the combined efforts of every individual you employ.
- Strategic management is based on upon answering three key questions:
  - What are my business's objectives?
  - What are the best ways to achieve those objectives?
  - What resources are required to make that happen?
- Once these steps have been taken, a strategic plan should begin to emerge — effectively setting the stage for answering the second question above, or "How best can we reach our goals?" Phase two of successful strategic management is formulating a plan by which the company can accomplish what it sets out to do. Therefore, strategic management is one part of IT Management.

16. Network Management
- Network management is the top-level administration and maintenance of large networks, often in areas such as computers or telecommunications, but not including user terminal equipment. In network management, functions such as security, monitoring, control, allocation, deployment, coordination and planning are executed.
- Security management is also a key component of network management. Security management protects a network from unauthorized access and includes many sub-functions, such as the authorization of subscriber access, control of the distribution of cryptographic keying material, and the distribution and reporting of security related events.
- Successful network management also uses accounting management. Accounting management controls and reports on the financial status of the network. This is done though analysis, planning, control of financial data reporting programs, and reporting for managerial decisions. This area of network management involves bank account maintenance, financial statement development, and analysis of cash flow and financial health.

17. Helpdesk Management
- Help desk typically provide a first line of assistance to users of IT systems. Technical support services are provided to assist and promote the use of technology within a business environment. The Help Desk is the traditional mechanism for these technical support services, usually accompanied by on-site assistance, training and self-help programs. Technical support can include many levels, including custom software assistance, off the shelf software assistance, hardware diagnostics, and related technical and training services.

- Help desks exist for one primary reason; to ensure a maximum return on the organizational investment in technology systems and services. In order to achieve this result, help desk services have to be effective, relevant and accessible.
- Helpdesks in order to be successful must know how to:
  - available
  - measurable
  - flexible
  - learn/teach

18. Application Management
- Application Management provides a methodology and tools that offer visibility into real-time metrics that help manage the key aspects of applications. Business Driven Application Management helps IT manage applications according to the needs of the business users so that valuable IT resources can be better focused to help deliver better business results.
- A company that does not appropriately manage the availability of its key software applications cannot remain competitive, and business suffers when enterprise applications do not perform as expected: lack of availability costs money.
- Application management may include;
  - Application life cycle management
  - Business Process management
  - Capacity Management
  - Financial Management
  - Portfolio Management
  - Development management
  - Deployment management

19. Knowledge Management
- In today's economy, knowledge is people, money, leverage, learning, flexibility, power, and competitive advantage. Knowledge is more relevant to sustained business than capital, labor or land. Nevertheless, it remains the most neglected asset. A holistic view considers knowledge to be present in ideas, judgments, talents, root causes, relationships, perspectives and concepts. Knowledge is stored in the individual brain or encoded in organizational processes, documents, products, services, facilities and systems. Knowledge management is an audit of "intellectual assets" that highlights unique sources, critical functions and potential bottlenecks which hinder knowledge flows to the point of use. It protects intellectual assets from decay, seeks opportunities to enhance decisions, services and products through adding intelligence, increasing value and providing flexibility.

20. Investment Management
- The business of investment management has several facets, including the employment of professional fund managers, research (of individual assets and asset classes), dealing, settlement, marketing, internal auditing, and the preparation of reports for clients.
- IT investment management has 3 phases;
    - Selection
- The organization selects those IT projects that will best support its mission needs and identifies and analyzes each project's risks and returns before committing significant funds to a project.
    - Screen
    - Rank
    - Select
    - Control
- The organization ensures that, as projects develop and as investment costs rise, the project is continuing to meet mission needs at the expected levels of cost and risk. If the project is not meeting expectations or if problems have arisen, steps are quickly taken to address the deficiencies.
    - Monitor progress
    - Take corrective action
    - Evaluate
- Actual versus expected results are compared once projects have been fully implemented. This is done to 1) assess the project's impact on mission performance, 2) identify any changes or modifications to the project that may be needed, and 3) revise the investment management process based on lessons learned.
    - Reviews
    - Adjustment
    - Apply lessons learned

21. Configuration Management
- Configuration management relates to both the security and quality areas of network management. It refers to the management of security features in a network by controlling changes made to the software, hardware, firmware, documentation, and test features in a system. This area of network management keeps the system under control as it evolves and grows, maintaining quality and security. Software configuration management can be divided into two main areas. The first is concerned with storage of entities from a software development project and is sometimes called component repository management. The second area involves production and change to these entities and is often referred to as engineering support.
- Computer hardware configuration goes beyond the recording of computer hardware for the purpose of asset management, although it can be used to maintain asset

information. The extra value provided is the rich source of support information that it provides to all interested parties. This information is typically stored together in a configuration management database (CMDB).
- The responsibilities of configuration management with regard to the CMDB are:
  - Identification
  - Control
  - Status accounting
  - Verification

22. Rights Management
- The purpose of this process is to grant authorized individuals the right to use a particular IT service while preventing access by unauthorized users. Access management executes the policies defined by information security management and availability management. Often, individuals are granted access to business applications using operating system, database and/or network "access control" mechanisms. Integrated business applications, however, are increasingly being held responsible for user and access management in service-oriented architectures that span technology boundaries to deliver functionality.
- In the areas of access management, any requirement to restrict the:
  1. Usage of application features or
  2. Access to business and personal information is part of "application security."

23. Life cycle Management
- Life cycle is consecutive and interlinked stages of a product system, from raw material acquisition or generation of natural resources to the final disposal. Life cycle management is an integrated concept for managing the total life cycle of goods and services towards more sustainable production and consumption.

24. IT Financial Management
- IT Financial Management is the discipline of ensuring that the IT infrastructure is obtained at the most effective price (which does not necessarily mean cheapest) and calculating the cost of providing IT services so that an organization can understand the costs of its IT services. These costs may then be recovered from the customer of the service.
- Costs are divided into costing units:
  - Equipment
  - Software
  - Organization (staff, overtime)
  - Accommodation
  - Transfer (costs of 3rd party service providers)

25. Security Management
- Security Management is the process of managing a defined level of security on information and IT services. Information security is achieved by implementing a

suitable set of controls, which could be policies, practices, procedures, organizational structures and software functions. These controls need to be established to ensure that the specific security objectives of the organization are met. (ISO17799:2000)

26. Content Management
- Content management consists of;
    - Web-based publishing: Documents and other forms of information can be published by authorized individuals. Page templates, wizards, and other software aids help inexperienced content authors to produce higher-quality output. Data useful on intranet, extranet, and ecommerce Internet sites, for example, can automatically be re-purposed and co-ordinate for the multiple destinations.
    - Format management: Data can automatically be converted into formats suitable for Web publishing such as HTML PDF. Legacy electronic documents, or even scanned paper documents, can be unified into a few common formats that are more easily shared with third parties.
    - Revision control: Files can be updated to a newer version or restored to a previous version. Changes to files can be traced to individuals for security purposes.
    - Indexing, search, and retrieval: For data to be valuable, it must be relevant to the task at hand and accessible in a timely fashion. Documents can be parsed for keywords, headings, graphics, and other elements; mechanisms for processing search requests become critical.
- More generally, effective content management systems support an organization's business processes for acquiring, filtering, organizing, and controlling access to information.

27. Risk Management
- As organizations use automated IT systems to process their information for better support of their missions, risk management plays a critical role in protecting an organization's information assets, and therefore its mission, from IT-related risk.
- An effective risk management process is an important component of a successful IT security program. The principal goal of an organization's risk management process should be to protect the organization and its ability to perform their mission, not just its IT assets. Therefore, the risk management process should not be treated primarily as a technical function carried out by the IT experts who operate and manage the IT system, but as an essential management function of the organization.
- Risk management is the process of identifying risk, assessing risk, and taking steps to reduce risk to an acceptable level. Risk management is the process that allows IT managers to balance the operational and economic costs of protective measures and achieve gains in mission capability by protecting the IT systems and data that support their organizations' missions.

28. Lean Management
- Lean Management is:
  - Defining the purpose of the organization in terms of customer value
  - Consumption problems of customers it is required to solve
  - Designing and executing the right value streams and processes for achieving the purpose and aligning the people touching the process and building problem solving capability in them It is now proven that Lean is applicable in any sphere of human activity, and a variety of industries –small and large from Retail, Office and Service industries have begun to appreciate the benefits of Lean Management and are transforming themselves. Many companies from Banking & Financial Services, Healthcare, Retail, Hospitality, BPOs, Call Centre & ITES and Software Industries have already embarked on a Lean management or are evaluating and seriously considering one. This is apart from Manufacturing Industries realizing that Lean Management is more than applying tools and techniques in the factory operations.

29. Resource Management
- In organizational studies, resource management is the efficient and effective deployment for an organization's resources when they are needed. Such resources may include financial resources, inventory, human skills, production resources, or information technology (IT). In the realm of project management, processes, techniques and philosophies as to the best approach for allocating resources have been developed.
- Core to this effort is learning how to optimize your resource utilization across all of IT – which ultimately will give you the planning flexibility you need to keep the right people on the right projects.
- Additionally, when faced with the all-too-common unplanned change request, you will know exactly what your trade-offs are and what choices you can offer your business customers. Making such informed choices will reduce the number of projects in jeopardy.
- A focus on achieving this type of strategic agility requires a shift from two predominant resource management approaches that have thus far impeded project management success rates:
  - Maintaining a narrow focus on time-tracking systems
  - Lack of workflow automation for key processes

30. Incident Management
- An incident is any event that is not part of the normal operation of an organization and causes a disruption of IT services. Within this context, incident management is the process to restore normal IT operations as quickly as possible to the organization

while minimizing the impact within defined service levels. It's important to note that incident management is about restoring service and not about resolving the underlying problem.
- Incident management programs that generally span five core areas:
  - Detection and recording
  - Classification, prioritization, and tracking
  - Investigation, escalation, and diagnosis
  - Resolution and recovery
  - Closure and communication
- While incident management can be a thankless job, it's a core process that every IT staff needs to master. Incident management identifies, classifies, and manages the resolution of incidents while minimizing their impact to the business. This role is critical in ensuring that the impact of IT incidents on the business is managed effectively.

31. Alert Management
- Alert management is a proven, valuable solution for the enterprise help desk. A good Alert management improves IT operations productivity by automating notification, assignment, collaboration, and resolution of IT incidents.

32. Capacity Management
- It is about ensuring that the right source levels are available where and when they are needed, at the right price. One view is that capacity management is about ensuring there is enough capacity, but it is equally about making sure there is not too much, with the unused resources incurring expense.

33. Patch Management
- The rise of widespread worms and malicious code targeting known vulnerabilities on unpatched systems, and the resultant downtime and expense they bring, is probably the biggest reason so any organizations are focusing on patch management. Along with these threats, increasing concern around governance and regulatory compliance has pushed enterprises to gain better control and oversight of their information assets.
- It's obvious that patch management is a critical issue. What is also clear is the main objective of a patch management program: to create a consistently configured environment that is secure against known vulnerabilities in operating system and application software. Unfortunately, as with many technology-based problems, good, practical solutions aren't as apparent. Managing updates for all the applications and operating system versions used in a small company is fairly complicated, and the

situation only becomes more complex when additional platforms, availability requirements, and remote offices and workers are factored in. A key component of patch management is the intake and vetting of information regarding both security issues and patch release - you must know which security issues and software updates are relevant to your environment.
- Several scheduling guidelines and plans should exist in a comprehensive patch management program.
- First, a patch cycle must exist that guides the normal application of patches and updates to systems. This cycle does not specifically target security or other critical updates. Instead, this patch cycle is meant to facilitate the application of standard patch releases and updates. After patch testing installation and deployment is where the actual work of applying patches and updates to production systems occurs. Audit, Consistency and Compliance checks must be done afterwards.

34. Role Management
- Role management helps you manage authorization, which enables you to specify the resources that users in your application are allowed to access. Role management lets you treat groups of users as a unit by assigning users to roles such as manager, sales, member, and so on.

35. Relationship Management
- Relation Management gives you the opportunity to register and manage all relevant information about your relations. Client Relationship Management is responsible for managing all aspects of ITS working relationships with clients to render high quality service delivery and to maximize client satisfaction.
- Client Relationship Management overall is comprised of four parts:
  - Understanding what the client is asking for, and needs.
  - Executing or delivering what the client is requesting.
  - Predicting what the client will need in the future.
  - Delivering targeted communications to respond to client needs.
- As part of a client-centric focus, the Client Relationship Management unit assesses all individual needs, aggregated into client segments, and organizational or unit needs. Business Relationship Management forms connection between the IT department and the business units it services. Business Relationship Management ensures that everyone is working at potential and that the most appropriate technologies are being used by the right people.

36. Portfolio Management
- IT portfolio management is the application of systematic management to large classes of items managed by enterprise IT capabilities. Examples of IT portfolios would be planned initiatives, projects, and ongoing IT services.

- IT Portfolio management is distinct from IT financial management in that it has an explicitly directive, strategic goal in determining what to continue investing in versus what to divest from. At its most mature, IT Portfolio management is accomplished through the creation of two portfolios:
  - Application portfolio
  - Project portfolio

37. Regulation Management
- The Computer Misuse Act 1990, enacted by Great Britain on 29 June 1990, and which came into force on 29 August 1990, is an example of one of the earliest of such legal enactments. This Act was enacted with an express purpose of making "provision for securing computer material against unauthorized access or modification".
- Certain major provisions of the Computer Misuse Act 1990 relate to:
  - "Unauthorized access to computer materials",
  - "Unauthorized access with intent to commit or facilitate the commission of further offences", and
  - "Unauthorized modification of computer material."
- The impact of the Computer Misuse Act 1990 has been limited and with the adoption of the Council of Europe adopts its Convention on Cyber-Crime, it has been indicated that amending legislation would be introduced in parliamentary session 2004-05 in order to rectify possible gaps in its coverage, which are many.
- In parallel with public opinion, governmental organizations have imposed stricter controls on companies. Regulations such as Sarbanes-Oxley, SEC Rule 17a-4, the Federal Rules of Civil Procedure, HIPPA ,and the European Union 8th Directive create business requirements for retaining key information assets. Failure to comply exposes companies to fines or regulatory sanctions so severe that non-complying organizations may cease to exist.
- In response to these new risks and shareholder pressures, many companies have enacted strict corporate governance policies – some more stringent than the regulations even require. As a result, organizations are keeping e-mails and certain types of files forever. By deploying strong business processes for archiving that are linked to larger corporate governance requirements, organizations can minimize business and legal risks.
- In Turkey, the law 5651 gives very broad authority to filter the net. It places this power in a single authority, as well as in the courts. It is unclear how broadly the law will be implemented. If the authority is well-meaning, as it seems to me to be, the effect of the law may be minimal; if that perspective changes, the effect of the law

could be dramatic. - The blocks are done at the domain level, it would appear. In other words, instead of blocking a single URL, the blocks affect entire domains. Many other states take this approach, probably for cost or efficiency reasons. Many states in the Middle East/North Africa have blocked entire blogging services at different times, for instance.
- The system in place requires Internet services to register themselves with the Turkish authorities (Middle East University). Internet Service Providers are themselves supposed to take the initiative to block access to content, which they then show to a judge who decides whether or not the blocking should continue. It will be will then be submitted to a "Communication Presidency," which like the "Telecommunication Council" is an entity specially created to ensure the new law's implementation.

38. Outsourcing Management
- Outsourcing is the process of contracting to a third-party. Organizations that outsource are seeking to realize benefits or address the following issues;
    - Cost savings
    - Focus on Core Business
    - Cost restructuring
    - Improve quality
    - Knowledge
    - Contract
    - Operational expertise
    - Access to talent
    - Capacity management
    - Risk management
    - Scalability

39. Asset Management
- Asset Management is a systematic process of operating, maintaining, and upgrading physical assets cost-effectively. It combines engineering and mathematical analyses with sound business practice and economic theory. IT asset management (ITAM) is the set of business practices that join financial, contractual and inventory functions to support life cycle management and strategic decision making for the IT environment.
- Types of Assets include:
    - Management
    - Organization
    - Process

- Knowledge
- People
- Information
- Applications
- Infrastructure
- Financial Capital

o The IT Asset Management function is the primary point of accountability for the life-cycle management of information technology assets throughout the organization. Included in this responsibility are development and maintenance of policies, standards, processes, systems and measurements that enable the organization to manage the IT Asset Portfolio with respect to risk, cost, control, IT Governance, compliance and business performance objectives as established by the business.

40. Archive Management

o There are many types of archives in the modern world. Libraries are archives of written works, museums are archives of physical objects, and national archives hold critical pieces of a nation's past. The discipline of maintaining archives or safeguarding critical objects is not a process limited to public service institutions. Businesses have maintained archives of corporate records and information for years. And in recent times, corporate governance and external regulations have mandated that businesses retain specific types of information assets. As a business process, archiving should link the requirements and goals of the business with the actions and tactics of its IT organization. Business Archive Management is a true business process that spans the entire organization to facilitate three goals: minimizing risk associated with governance concerns, enabling the efficient use of corporate assets, and generating value through the reuse of information assets.

o The three key drivers of Business Archive Management are the need for corporate governance, efficient use of corporate assets, and business reuse of information. Business Archive Management requires mastering four core capabilities:
- Business planning
- Archive planning and design
- Archive operations and support
- Infrastructure management

■■■

Chapter 5...

Understanding the Business Values of System and Managing Change

Contents ...

5.1 The Importance of Project Management
    5.1.1 Runaway Projects and System Failure
    5.1.2 Project Management Objectives
5.2 Establishing the Business Value of Information Systems
    5.2.1 Information System Costs and Benefits
    5.2.2 Capital Budgeting for Information Systems
5.3 Case Example: Capital Budgeting for a new Supply Chain Management System
    5.3.1 Accounting Rate of Return on Investment (ROI)
    5.3.2 Internal Rate of Return (IRR)
    5.3.3 Results of the Capital Budgeting Analysis
    5.3.4 Real Options Pricing Models
    5.3.5 Limitations of Financial Models
5.4 Organisational Change
    5.4.1 Meaning of Organisational Change
    5.4.2 Levels of Change
    5.4.3 Types of Change
    5.4.4 Resistance to Change
    5.4.5 Kurt Lewin's Force Field Analysis Change Model
5.5 Change Management in Information System Development and Implementation Projects
    5.5.1 Change management
    5.5.2 Organisational changes
    5.5.3 Resistance to change
    5.5.4 Organisational Culture

5.1 The Importance of Project Management

- There is a very high failure rate among information systems projects. In nearly every organization, information systems projects take much more time and money to implement than originally anticipated, or the completed system does not work properly.

When an information system fails to work properly or costs too much to develop, companies may not realize any benefit from their information system investment, and the system may not be able to solve the problems for which it was intended. The development of a new system must be carefully managed and orchestrated, and the way a project is executed is likely to be the most important factor influencing its outcome. That's why it's essential to have some knowledge about how to manage information systems projects and about how and why they succeed or fail.

5.1.1 Runaway Projects and System Failure

- How badly are projects managed? On average, private sector projects are underestimated by one-half in terms of budget and time required to deliver the complete system promised in the system plan. A very large number of projects are delivered with missing functionality. The Standish Group consultancy, which monitors IT project success rates, found that only 29 percent of all technology investments were completed on time, on budget, and with all features and functions originally specified. Between 30 and 40 percent of all software projects are "runaway" projects that far exceed the original schedule and budget projections and fail to perform as originally specified.
- A systems development project without proper management will most likely suffer these consequences:
    - Costs that greatly exceed budgets
    - Unexpected time slippage
    - Technical performance that is less than expected
    - Failure to obtain anticipated benefits
- The systems produced by failed information projects are often not used in the way they were intended, or they are not used at all. Users often have to develop parallel manual systems to make these systems work.
- The actual design of the system may fail to capture essential business requirements or improve organizational performance. Information may not be provided quickly enough to be helpful; it may be in a format that is impossible to digest and use; or it may represent the wrong pieces of data.
- The way in which nontechnical business users must interact with the system may be excessively complicated and discouraging. A system may be designed with a poor user interface. The user interface is the part of the system with which end users interact. For example, an online input form or data entry screen may be so poorly arranged that no one wants to submit data or request information. System outputs may be displayed in a format that is too difficult to comprehend.
- Web sites may discourage visitors from exploring further if the Web pages are cluttered and poorly arranged, if users cannot easily find the information they are seeking, or if it takes too long to access and display the Web page on the user's computer.

- Additionally, the data in the system may have a high level of inaccuracy or inconsistency. The information in certain fields may be erroneous or ambiguous, or it may not be organized properly for business purposes. Information required for a specific business function may be inaccessible because the data are incomplete.

5.1.2 Project Management Objectives

- A project is a planned series of related activities for achieving a specific business objective. Information systems projects include the development of new information systems, enhancing existing systems, or projects for replacing or upgrading the firm's information technology (IT) infrastructure.
- Project management refers to the application of knowledge, skills, tools, and techniques to achieve specific targets within specified budget and time constraints. Project management activities include planning the work, assessing risk, estimating resources required to accomplish the work, organizing the work, acquiring human and material resources, assigning tasks, directing activities, controlling project execution, reporting progress, and analyzing the results. As in other areas of business, project management for information systems must deal with five major variables: scope, time, cost, quality, and risk.
- Scope defines what work is or is not included in a project. For example, the scope of project for a new order processing system might include new modules for inputting orders and transmitting them to production and accounting but not any changes to related accounts receivable, manufacturing, distribution, or inventory control systems. Project management defines all the work required to complete a project successfully, and should ensure that the scope of a project not expand beyond what was originally intended.
- Time is the amount of time required to complete the project. Project management typically establishes the amount of time required to complete major components of a project. Each of these components is further broken down into activities and tasks. Project management tries to determine the time required to complete each task and establish a schedule for completing the work.
- Cost is based on the time to complete a project multiplied by the cost of human resources required to complete the project. Information systems project costs also include the cost of hardware, software, and work space. Project management develops a budget for the project and monitors ongoing project expenses.
- Quality is an indicator of how well the end result of a project satisfies the objectives specified by management. The quality of information systems projects usually boils down to improved organizational performance and decision making. Quality also considers the accuracy and timeliness of information produced by the new system and ease of use.

- Risk refers to potential problems that would threaten the success of a project. These potential problems might prevent a project from achieving its objectives by increasing time and cost, lowering the quality of project outputs, or preventing the project from being completed altogether.

5.2 Establishing the Business Value of Information Systems

- Even if a system project supports a firm's strategic goals and meets user information requirements, it needs to be a good investment for the firm. The value of systems from a financial perspective essentially revolves around the issue of return on invested capital. Does a particular information system investment produce sufficient returns to justify its costs?

5.2.1 Information System Costs and Benefits

- Tangible benefits can be quantified and assigned a monetary value. Intangible benefits, such as more efficient customer service or enhanced decision making, cannot be immediately quantified but may lead to quantifiable gains in the long run. Transaction and clerical systems that displace labor and save space always produce more measurable, tangible benefits than management information systems, decision-support systems, and computer-supported collaborative work systems.
- Chapter 5 introduced the concept of total cost of ownership (TCO), which is designed to identify and measure the components of information technology expenditures beyond the initial cost of purchasing and installing hardware and software. However, TCO analysis provides only part of the information needed to evaluate an information technology investment because it does not typically deal with benefits, cost categories such as complexity costs, and "soft" and strategic factors discussed later in this section.

5.2.2 Capital Budgeting for Information Systems

- Capital budgeting models are one of several techniques used to measure the value of investing in long-term capital investment projects. Firms invest in capital projects to expand production to meet anticipated demand or to modernize production equipment to reduce costs. Firms also invest in capital projects for many noneconomic reasons, such as installing pollution control equipment, converting to a human resources database to meet some government regulations, or satisfying nonmarket public demands. Information systems are considered long-term capital investment projects.
- The principal capital budgeting models for evaluating information technology projects are:
    - The payback method
    - The accounting rate of return on investment (ROI)
    - The net present value
    - The internal rate of return (IRR)

Table 5.1: Costs and Benefits of Information Systems

COSTS
Hardware
Telecommunications
Software
Services
Personnel
TANGIBLE BENEFITS (COST SAVINGS)
Increased productivity
Lower operational costs
Reduced workforce
Lower computer expenses
Lower outside vendor costs
Lower clerical and professional costs
Reduced rate of growth in expenses
Reduced facility costs
INTANGIBLE BENEFITS
Improved asset utilization
Improved resource control
Improved organizational planning
Increased organizational flexibility
More timely information
More information
Increased organizational learning
Legal requirements attained
Enhanced employee goodwill
Increased job satisfaction
Improved decision making
Improved operations
Higher client satisfaction
Better corporate image

- Capital budgeting methods rely on measures of cash flows into and out of the firm. Capital projects generate cash flows into and out of the firm. The investment cost for information systems projects is an immediate cash outflow caused by expenditures for hardware, software, and labor. In subsequent years, the investment may cause additional cash outflows that will be balanced by cash inflows resulting from the investment. Cash inflows take the form of increased sales of more products (for reasons such as new products, higher quality, or increasing market share) or reduced costs in production and operations. The difference between cash outflows and cash inflows is used for calculating the financial worth of an investment. Once the cash flows have been established, several alternative methods are available for comparing different projects and deciding about the investment.

5.3 Case Example: Capital Budgeting for a new Supply Chain Management System

- Let's look at how financial models would work in a real-world business scenario. Heartland Stores is a general merchandise retail chain operating in eight Midwestern states. It has 5 regional distribution centers, 377 stores, and about 14,000 different products stocked in each store. The company is considering investing in new software and hardware modules to upgrade its existing supply chain management system to help it better manage the purchase and movement of goods from its suppliers to its retail outlets. Too many items in Heartland's stores are out of stock, even though many of these products are in the company's distribution center warehouses.

- Management believes that the new system would help Heartland Stores reduce the amount of items that it must stock in inventory, and thus its inventory costs, because it would be able to track precisely the status of orders and the flow of items in and out of its distribution centers. The new system would reduce Heartland's labor costs because the company would not need so many people to manage inventory or to track shipments of goods from suppliers to distribution centers and from distribution centers to retail outlets. Telecommunications costs would be reduced because customer service representatives and shipping and receiving staff would not have to spend so much time on the telephone tracking shipments and orders. Heartland Stores expects the system to reduce transportation costs by providing information to help it consolidate shipments to retail stores and to create more efficient shipping schedules. If the new system project is approved, implementation would commence in January 2007 and the new system would become operational in early January 2008.

- The solution builds the existing IT infrastructure at the Heartland Stores but requires the purchase of additional server computers, PCs, database software, and networking technology, along with new supply chain planning and execution software. The solution also calls for new radio-frequency identification technology to track items more easily as they move from suppliers to distribution centers to retail outlets.

- Fig. 5.1 shows the estimated costs and benefits of the system. The system had an actual investment cost of $11,467,350 in the first year (year 0) and a total cost over six years of $19,017,350. The estimated benefits total $32,500,000 after six years. Was the investment worthwhile?

The Payback Method

- The payback method is quite simple: It is a measure of the time required to pay back the initial investment of a project. The payback period is computed as follows:

$$\frac{\text{Original investment}}{\text{Annual net cash inflow}} = \text{Number of years to pay back}$$

- In the case of Heartland Stores, it will take more than two years to pay back the initial investment. (Because cash flows are uneven, annual cash inflows are summed until they equal the original investment to arrive at this number.) The payback method is a popular method because of its simplicity and power as an initial screening method. It is especially good for high-risk projects in which the useful life of a project is difficult to determine. If a project pays for itself in two years, then it matters less how long after two years the system lasts.

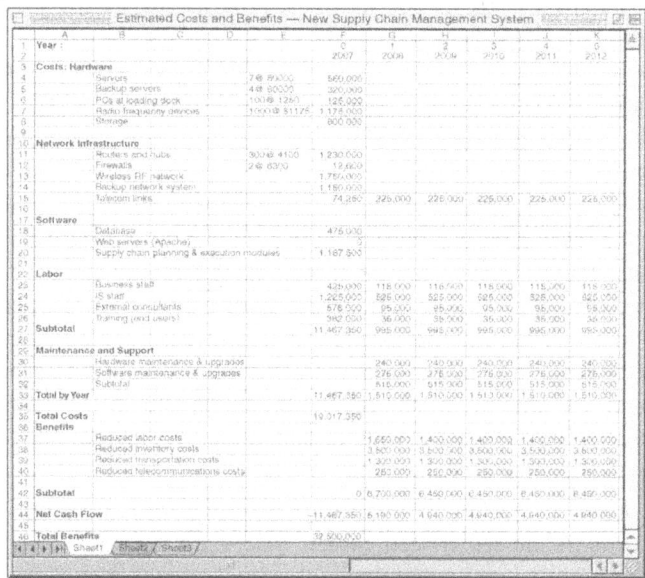

Fig. 5.1: Costs and Benefits of the New Supply Chain Management System

This spreadsheet analyzes the basic costs and benefits of implementing supply chain management system enhancements for a midsize midwestern U.S. retailer. The costs for hardware, telecommunications, software, services, and personnel are analyzed over a six-year period.

- The weakness of this measure is its virtue: The method ignores the time value of money, the amount of cash flow after the payback period, the disposal value (usually zero with computer systems), and the profitability of the investment.

IT in Management — Understanding the Business Values of System and Managing Change

5.3.1 Accounting Rate of Return on Investment (ROI)

- Firms make capital investments to earn a satisfactory rate of return. Determining a satisfactory rate of return depends on the cost of borrowing money, but other factors can enter into the equation. Such factors include the historic rates of return expected by the firm. In the long run, the desired rate of return must equal or exceed the cost of capital in the marketplace. Otherwise, no one will lend the firm money.

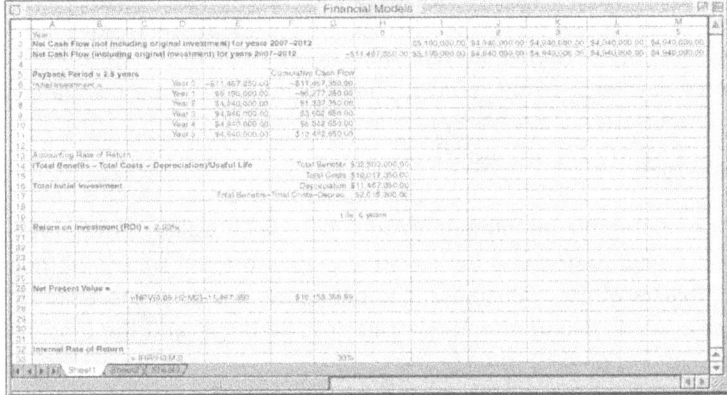

Fig. 5.2: Financial Models

To determine the financial basis for an information systems project, a series of financial models helps determine the return on invested capital. These calculations include the payback period, the accounting rate of return on investment (ROI), the net present value, and the internal rate of return (IRR).

- The accounting rate of return on investment (ROI) calculates the rate of return from an investment by adjusting the cash inflows produced by the investment for depreciation. It gives an approximation of the accounting income earned by the project.
- To find the ROI, first calculate the average net benefit. The formula for the average net benefit is as follows:

$$\frac{\text{(Total benefits} - \text{Total cost} - \text{Depreciation)}}{\text{Useful life}} = \text{Net benefit}$$

- This net benefit is divided by the total initial investment to arrive at ROI. The formula is as follows:

$$\frac{\text{Net benefit}}{\text{Total initial investment}} = \text{ROI}$$

- In the case of Heartland Stores, the average rate of return on the investment is 2.93 percent.
- The weakness of ROI is that it can ignore the time value of money. Future savings are simply not worth as much in today's dollars as are current savings. However, ROI can be modified (and usually is) so that future benefits and costs are calculated in today's dollars. (The present value function on most spreadsheets can perform this conversion.)

Net Present Value

- Evaluating a capital project requires that the cost of an investment (a cash outflow usually in year 0) be compared with the net cash inflows that occur many years later. But these two kinds of cash flows are not directly comparable because of the time value of money. Money you have been promised to receive three, four, and five years from now is not worth as much as money received today. Money received in the future has to be discounted by some appropriate percentage rate—usually the prevailing interest rate, or sometimes the cost of capital. Present value is the value in current dollars of a payment or stream of payments to be received in the future. It can be calculated by using the following formula:

$$\text{Payment} \times \frac{1 - (1 + 1 \text{ interest})^{-11}}{\text{Interest}} = \text{Present value}$$

- Thus, to compare the investment (made in today's dollars) with future savings or earnings, you need to discount the earnings to their present value and then calculate the net present value of the investment. The net present value is the amount of money an investment is worth, taking into account its cost, earnings, and the time value of money. The formula for net present value is this:

- Present value of expected cash flows − Initial investment cost = Net present value

- In the case of Heartland Stores, the present value of the stream of benefits is $21,625,709, and the cost (in today's dollars) is $11,467,350, giving a net present value of $10,158,359. In other words, for a $21 million investment today, the firm will receive more than $10 million. This is a fairly good rate of return on an investment.

5.3.2 Internal Rate of Return (IRR)

- Internal rate of return (IRR) is defined as the rate of return or profit that an investment is expected to earn, taking into account the time value of money. IRR is the discount (interest) rate that will equate the present value of the project's future cash flows to the initial cost of the project (defined here as negative cash flow in year 0 of $11,467,350). In other words, the value of R (discount rate) is such that Present value − Initial cost = 0. In the case of Heartland Stores, the IRR is 33 percent.

5.3.3 Results of the Capital Budgeting Analysis

- Using methods that take into account the time value of money, the Heartland Stores project is cash-flow positive over the time period under consideration and returns more benefits than it costs. Against this analysis, you might ask what other investments would be better from an efficiency and effectiveness standpoint and if all the benefits have been calculated.

5.3.4 Real Options Pricing Models

- Some information systems projects are highly uncertain, especially investments in IT infrastructure. Their future revenue streams are unclear and their up-front costs are high. Suppose, for instance, that a firm is considering a $20 million investment to upgrade its information technology infrastructure—its hardware, software, data management tools, and networking technology. If this upgraded infrastructure were available, the organization would have the technology capabilities to respond more easily to future problems and opportunities. Although the costs of this investment can be calculated, not all of the benefits of making this investment can be established in advance. But if the firm waits a few years until the revenue potential becomes more obvious, it might be too late to make the infrastructure investment. In such cases, managers might benefit from using real options pricing models to evaluate information technology investments.

- **Real options pricing models (ROPMs)** use the concept of options valuation borrowed from the financial industry. An option is essentially the right, but not the obligation, to act at some future date. A typical call option, for instance, is a financial option in which a person buys the right (but not the obligation) to purchase an underlying asset (usually a stock) at a fixed price (strike price) on or before a given date. For instance, on June 5, 2006, for $8.70 you could purchase the right (a call option) maturing in January 2008 to buy a share of Procter & Gamble (P&G) common stock for $50 per share. If, by the end of January 2008, the price of P&G stock did not rise above $50 per share, you would not exercise the option, and the value of the option would fall to zero on the strike date. If, however, the price of Procter & Gamble common stock rose to, say, $100 per share, you could purchase the stock for the strike price of $50 and retain the profit of $50 per share minus the cost of the option. (Because the option is sold as a 100-share contract, the cost of the contract would be 100 × $8.70 before commissions, or $870, and you would be purchasing and obtaining a profit from 100 shares of Procter & Gamble.) The stock option enables the owner to benefit from the upside potential of an opportunity while limiting the downside risk.

- ROPMs value information systems projects similar to stock options, where an initial expenditure on technology creates the right, but not the obligation, to obtain the benefits associated with further development and deployment of the technology as long as management as the freedom to cancel, defer, restart, or expand the project. ROPMs give managers the flexibility to stage their IT investment or test the waters with small pilot projects or prototypes to gain more knowledge about the risks of a project before investing in the entire implementation. The disadvantages of this model are primarily in estimating all the key variables affecting option value, including anticipated cash flows from the underlying asset and changes in the cost of implementation. Models for determining option value of information technology platforms are being developed.

5.3.5 Limitations of Financial Models

- The traditional focus on the financial and technical aspects of an information system tends to overlook the social and organizational dimensions of information systems that may affect the true costs and benefits of the investment. Many companies' information systems investment decisions do not adequately consider costs from organizational disruptions created by a new system, such 572 Part Four Building and Managing Systems as the cost to train end users, the impact that users' learning curves for a new system have on productivity, or the time managers need to spend overseeing new system-related changes. Benefits, such as more timely decisions from a new system or enhanced employee learning and expertise, may also be overlooked in a traditional financial analysis.

5.4 Organisational Change

The real world is turbulent, requiring organisations and their members to undergo dynamic change if they are to perform at competitive levels.

If environments were perfectly static, if employees' skills and abilities were always up to date and incapable of deteriorating, and if tomorrows were exactly same as today, organisation change would have little or no importance for managers.

Managers are the primary change agents in most organisations and they shape the organisation's change culture through the decisions they make and by their role-modeling behaviour.

Management decisions related to structural designs, cultural factors, and human resource policies largely determine the level of innovation within the organisation. Management decisions, policies and practices will determine the degree to which the organisation learns and adapts to changing environmental factors.

5.4.1 Meaning of Organisational Change

In the modern business environment, organisations face rapid change like never before. Globalisation and the constant innovation of technology result in a constantly evolving business environment. Phenomena such as social media and mobile adaptability have revolutionised business and the effect of this, is an ever increasing, need for change and therefore change management.

Organisation change occurs when business strategies or major sections of an organisation are altered. Also, known as, reorganisation, restructuring and turnaround.

Organisational change is a structured approach in an organisation for ensuring that changes are smoothly and successfully implemented to achieve lasting benefits.

Due to globalisation, the modern business environment is changing rapidly and so is the technology. Organisations have to face these changes constantly. Emergence of various new trends such as social media and mobile applications has brought in revolutionary changes in the way businesses operate today. Organisations are also said to have changed when they change their business strategies or major divisions. These are termed as reorganisation, restructuring and turnaround.

All this has resulted into the need for change management for most of the organisations. Organisational change is a structured approach undertaken to ensure that changes are introduced smoothly and implemented successfully to survive in the evolving business environment and gain a competitive advantage over others.

Organisations must be able to deal with the changes comfortably and hence the ability of managers to manage and adapt to organisational change has become crucial today.

Organisational change affects all the departments and all the levels in an organisation directly. Thus the entire company must learn how to handle changes in the organisation.

5.4.2 Levels of Change

Change can be at individual, group and organisational level.

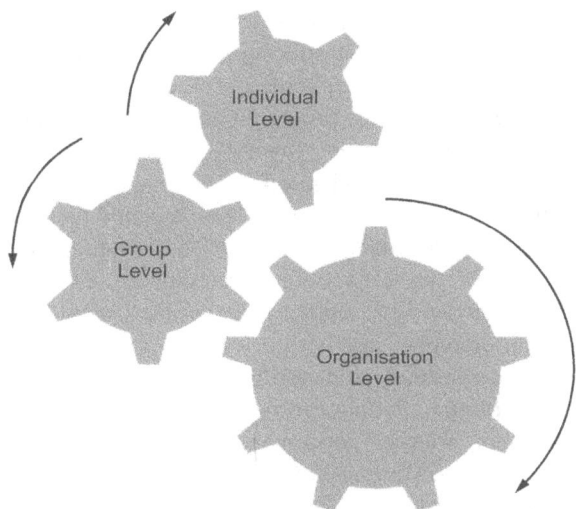

Fig. 5.3: Levels of Change

1. **Individual Level Change:** At the individual level, change is reflected in developments such as changes in a job assignment, physical move to a different location or the changes in maturity of a person which occurs over time. Changes at the individual level will have significant implication for the total organisation. A manager, who desires to implement a major change at the individual level, transferring an employee for instance, must understand that the change will have repercussions beyond the individual.

2. **Group Level Change:** Most organisations implement change at the group level. It is because of group activity. The group could be departments or informal work groups. Changes at the group level can affect work, efficiency and behaviour at the work and social organisation and status system.

   Managers should take groups into consideration while bringing change into the system however informal groups can pose a major barrier because they have majority of strength. Formal groups can resist change by the way of unions.

3. **Organisational Change:** Changes at this level involve major programmes that affect both individuals and groups. Such decisions are made at the top level. It requires longer duration and detailed planning to implement this change.

5.4.3 Types of Change

(A) Changes Related to People

1. **Personnel Change:** Sometimes changes are a direct result of other organisational changes. Or else, companies simply seek to change worker's attitudes and behaviours in order to increase their effectiveness. **Bateman** and **Zeithaml** suggest that attempting a strategic change, introducing a new technology and other changes in the work environment may affect people's attitudes (sometimes in a negative way). Frequently, management initiates programmes with a conscious goal of directly and positively changing the people themselves. The science of organisational development deals with changing people. This may be done on the job through techniques such as education and training, team building and career planning.

2. **Culture Change:** Culture change within an organisation aims at changing the behaviour patterns of the organisation's employees. Some examples of culture change include reward-and-recognition programmes, employee empowerment and training. These programmes attempt to improve motivation and decision-making skills and to increase sensitivity to diversity issues.

3. **People-centred Change:** People-centred process changes attempt to alter the attitudes, behaviours, skills or performance of employees within an organisation. Communication, employee motivation, leadership and group interaction are some primary focuses of people-centred change. This type of change may affect the employees and their behaviours in many areas. Some examples are: improved problem-solving skills, the way employees learn new skills, and how employees perceive themselves, their jobs and the organisation.

4. **Social Change:** Social change refers to the modification of established relationships in the organisation. Social change encompasses the large set of goals that organisations establish around people. This includes an empowered workforce, collaborative work arrangements and matching personal fulfilment to organisational needs.

(B) Changes Related to Organisations
1. **Leadership Change:** Leadership transitions are critical. Transitions in leadership offer an opportunity to make changes in many areas of the organisation. The situation is fluid or, in Lewin's framework of organisational change, 'unfrozen.' "The transition is an occasion to rethink the commitment to the present agenda, to reflect on roads not taken in the past and to review future choices. Many significant changes – in policy, people, organisational structure and procedures – are more easily introduced simultaneously with a leadership change.
2. **Structural Change:** Changes within an organisation's structure can occur due to external influences. Structural changes may involve structural characteristics, administrative procedures or management systems. They may involve simple policy changes or be as complex as a complete restructuring of the management hierarchy.
3. **Reengineering:** Change centred on reengineering focuses on making major structural changes in the organisation. Implementation of these changes typically focus on everyday tasks or procedures. The goal is to substantially improve productivity, efficiency, quality and customer satisfaction.
4. **Incremental Organisational Change:** Incremental change is a step-by-step approach to re-designing an organisation. Each small increment that is changed produces changes in other parts of the organisation. By changing specific processes or portions, the entire organisation changes over time.
5. **Fundamental Organisational Change:** When major organisational changes are necessary and time constraints are a significant factor, a more radical transformation becomes essential. Fundamental organisational change focuses on changing major characteristics of the entire organisation rather than specific parts.
6. **Paradigm Shift:** Sometimes the basic rules of the game shift and such shift is not predetermined. Some people and companies simply start to work with it and begin to achieve new levels of success. This phenomenon is known as a "paradigm shift." Many people use the term loosely - but very few actually understand it until it becomes the brick wall that stands in the way of progress.
7. **Strategic Change:** Strategic changes involve long-term planning while incorporating a strong external orientation. These changes may cover major functional areas of an organisation. This type of change may occur while adjusting the firm's strategy to achieve the goals of the company. This type of change may also result in a change to the mission statement of the organisation. An organisation's approach to doing business, targeted markets, partnerships or the types of products sold may be included in the strategic change approach.

(C) Changes Related to Systems

1. **Process-oriented Change:** The goal of process-oriented change is to improve productivity. Process-oriented change affects the way in which an organisation delivers services, produces products and handles current business practices. As the environmental factors of an organisation change, the need for process-oriented change increases.

2. **Technological Change:** This type of approach concerns the implementation or integration of technology into the processes of an organisation. Primarily, technology includes large hardware or software systems.

3. **Systems Change:** Systems change means making a change that endures and changes the heart of the organisation. Such change is systematic and needs time, planning and patience. It is not done by just tweaking parts of the system in isolation. But, it means ultimately impacting change across all elements of the system.

4. **Continuous Improvement:** Continuous improvement entails finding the best practices, adapting them and continually improving them. When using these ideas to encourage constant improvement; new product and service ideas, new processes, and opportunities for growth become the norm.

    The process of continuous improvement occurs by developing a series of measureable processes. The next step is to acknowledge and correct defects.

5. **Continual Change:** Continual change is similar to continuous process improvement but is a broader term. This builds on the philosophy that when change stops, companies cease to exist. Continual change to optimise technological breakthroughs is required for an organisation to systemically evolve. This change continues until it has exhausted the improvement that is known.

6. **Transactional Change:** Transactional change occurs in a situation in which the organisation experiences some feature of change but the fundamental nature of the organisation remains the same. This may include a company's organisational climate, which encompasses the perceptions and attitudes of people about the organisation. Transactional change includes changes to structure, management practices and systems.

7. **Business Process Reengineering:** Business process reengineering is the redesign of business processes and the associated systems and organisational structures. The goal of this type of change is to achieve a dramatic improvement in business performance.

(D) Change in General

1. **Growth:** Growth needs to be managed on multiple levels i.e. the right leaders, leading the right people, to do the right things, at the right time.

2. **Unplanned Change:** Unplanned change usually occurs because of a major and sudden surprise to the organisation. This causes its members to respond in a highly reactive and disorganised fashion.

   At times, organisational change happens when it becomes necessary to react to a sudden development. Emergency can force organisations to introduce new ways of doing things or to restructure themselves.

3. **Planned Change:** Planned change occurs when leaders in the organisation recognise the need for a major change and proactively organise a plan to accomplish the change. Planned change occurs with successful implementation of a strategic plan, reorganisation plan or other types of plan for implementation of a change of this magnitude.

4. **Radical Change:** Radical change is a process by which firms regain competitive advantage after it has been lost or threatened significantly. The type and extent of change undertaken depends upon the firm's resources and capabilities, its competitive environment and its leadership. Radical change is divergent and meant to fundamentally change the firm's processes, systems, structures, strategies and core values.

5. **Developmental Change:** Developmental change concentrates on improving an already successful environment. Development occurs through improving aspects of an organisation such as increasing customer base or introducing a product expansion.

6. **Transformational Change:** Transformational change occurs when organisations implement drastic changes and essentially transform themselves. This can occur when an organisation faces different technologies, significant changes in supply and demand, unexpected competition, lack of revenue or other major shifts in the way they do business.

   Transformational change is where the organisation is fundamentally and substantially altered. Organisational culture is part of transformational change and is harder to change as against organisational climate because of its deeply-rooted beliefs and values. Included in transformational change are mission and strategy, leadership and organisational culture.

7. **Transitional Change:** Transitional change involves the replacement of a current process with a process that is new to the company. Mergers, acquisitions, new product creation and the implementation of new technologies are examples of transitional change.

Transitional change requires the introduction of new processes that modify the way the company operates, in the event that current methods of operation are no longer applicable. Examples of transitional change include reorganisation, minor restructuring, utilisation of new operational techniques / methods / procedures or the introduction of new services or products.

8. **Strategy Deployment:** These projects are defined as building or changing the capabilities of the organisation. Some efforts involve trying to improve what the organisation does and other efforts involve creating radically new strengths.
9. **Restructuring / Downsizing:** These projects involve rearranging organisational units and / or the workforce. Downsizing primarily refers to reducing the number of employees and it also includes divestiture of company assets, that is, selling off a piece of the business. It is based upon quantitative measure of operational and financial performance.
10. **Remedial Change:** Remedial change addresses a particular situation, which needs immediate attention. For example, a deficiency in a product line or employee burnout. It is said to be successful when there is a solution to the problem.
11. **Evolutionary Change:** Evolutionary change involves setting direction, allocating responsibilities and establishing reasonable timelines for achieving objectives. However it is not fast enough or comprehensive enough to move ahead of the curve, in an evolving world, where stakes are high and the response time is short.
12. **Revolutionary Change:** When faced with market-driven urgency, abrupt and sometimes disruptive changes happen. Dramatic downsizing or reengineering may be required to keep the company competitive. In situations where time is critical to success and companies must become more efficient and productive rapidly, revolutionary change is demanded.
13. **Proactive Change:** Proactive change involves actively attempting to make alterations to the work place and its practices. Companies that take a proactive approach to change often try to avoid a potential future threat or to capitalise on a potential future opportunity.
14. **Reactive Change:** Reactive change occurs when an organisation makes changes in its practices after the occurrence of some threat or opportunity.

Forces for Change
1. **Organisations face a dynamic and changing environment:** This requires adaptation. Six specific forces that are acting as stimulants for change are limited focus to change, threat to expertise, group inertia, structural inertia, threat to established power relationships, threat to established resource allocation.

2. **The changing nature of the workforce:**
   - A multicultural environment.
   - Human resource policies and practices changed to attract and keep this more diverse workforce.
   - Large expenditure on training to upgrade reading, math, computer, and other skills of employees
3. **Technology is changing jobs and organisations:**
   - Sophisticated information technology is also making organisations more responsive. As organisations have had to become more adaptable, so too have their employees.
   - We live in an "age of discontinuity." Beginning in the early 1970s with the overnight quadrupling of world oil prices, economic shocks have continued to impose changes on organisations.
4. **Competition is changing:**
   - The global economy means global competitors.
   - Established organisations need to defend themselves against both traditional competitors and small, entrepreneurial firms with innovative offerings.
   - Successful organisations will be the ones that can change in response to the competition.
5. **Social trends during the past generation suggest changes that organisations have to adjust for:**
   - The expansion of the Internet, Baby Boomers retiring, and people moving from the suburbs back to cities.
   - A global context for OB is required. No one could have imagined how world politics would change in recent years.
   - September 11th has caused changes organisations have made in terms of practices concerning security, back-up systems, employee stereotyping, etc.

5.4.4 Resistance to Change

- Resistance to change is understood to be a natural phenomenon. But not all changes are resisted. In many organisations changes are accepted instead of being resisted. People have a natural instinct to accept change. Sources of resistance to change may be **rational or emotional.** Rational resistance occurs when people do not have proper information about the change.
- Emotional resistance is the feeling of resistance to change evoked due to the people's perception of how the change will affect them.
- Resistance to change is normal and people cling to habits and to the status quo. Managerial actions can minimise or arouse resistance. People must be motivated to get

away from old habits. This must take place in stages rather than abruptly so that "managed change" takes on the character of "natural change." In addition to normal inertia, organisation change introduces anxieties about the future. If the future after the change is perceived positively, resistance will be less.
- Education and communication are therefore key ingredients in minimising negative reactions.
- Employees can be informed about both the nature of the change and the logic behind it before it takes place through reports, memos, group presentations or individual discussions. Another important component of overcoming resistance is inviting employee participation and involvement, in both the design and implementation phases of the change effort. Organised forms of facilitation and support can be deployed. Managers can ensure that employees will have the resources to bring about the change; they can make themselves available to provide explanations and to minimise stress arising in many situations.

Reasons for Resistance to Change
- The basic problem in the management of change is the study of reasons for resistance to change. Change is a persistent phenomenon, but people resist change in the context of their pattern of life or in the context of their situations in the organisation. Change of any type demands readjustment while it is not simple, possible and favourable to all. Hence, resistance to change is also very usual like the change itself.

(A) Economic Causes
1. **Fear of Losing Job or Reduction in Employment:** Due to the change in technology, methods of work, use of automatic machines and quantity or quality of work required; people think that there will be a reduction in their employment opportunities, as they will not be able to cope up with the machines. This fear leads to resistance to change on the part of the workers.
2. **Insecurity of Job:** Generally, change in technology is expected to result in technical unemployment, as old employees may not be able to handle new machines. Hence the fear of unemployment leads to resistance to change. Such resistance is individual as well as collective.
3. **Doubt about Future or Fear of Obsolescence:** Employees may fear that they may be demoted, if they do not possess the new skills required for their jobs, after the introduction of change. There is uncertainty of adjustment, separation of group etc. Hence, they prefer status-quo positions.
4. **Fear and Increased Work Load:** Change in work technology and methods may result in the fear that work-load will be increased, while there will be no corresponding increase in their remuneration. This feeling results in resistance to change.

(B) Personal Causes
1. **Requirement of Training:** If due to changes in technology and work, the organisation requires training and relearning for employees, it may lead to resistance as all persons may not like to undergo refreshers and training courses.
2. **Boredom and Monotony:** If the proposed change is expected to lead to greater specialisation resulting in boredom and monotony, it may also be resisted by people.
3. **Non-involvement in Decision-making:** If employees are not allowed to take part in the decision-making process for change, then they may resist the change. When they do not fully understand the implications of change, they resist it. Some employees resist change as it implies a criticism of the present methods as inadequate or unsuitable for which they may not agree.

(C) Social Causes
1. **Need for New Social Adjustment:** Any organisational change requires new social adjustments with the group, work situation and new employer. All individuals are not ready to accept this challenge. Some people even refuse promotions on this ground as they may have to break their present social contacts.
2. **Taking Change as Pressure of Outside Power:** Some employees take any change as imposed from outside upon them. This happens particularly when change is brought about abruptly. If employees are consulted and given due participation in the process of introducing change; their objection and resistance can be minimised.
3. **Orthodox Mentality:** Some employees consider that every change is for the benefit of the management and enterprise itself, rather than the benefits of employees or even the general public. Hence, they resist change.

Overcoming Resistance to Change
- Management is responsible for bringing various changes. Hence, it acts as an agent for the changes. If the management has to introduce change slowly and successfully in the organisation, it has to overcome the resistance and make it a successful venture. An atmosphere for change is to be created. The management must realise that resistance to change is basically a human problem, though on surface, it may appear to be related to technical aspects of change. So, it must be tackled in a human and social manner. In short, the following steps can be taken by management to facilitate change acceptance.
    1. **Discussion about the Changes with Workers/Employees:** Before introducing any change, the employees should be fully consulted and they must be made a party to any such decision. The meaning and purpose of the change must be fully communicated to those who will be affected by it. Sufficient time should be allowed for discussion and for inviting their suggestions.

2. **Proper Planning for Change:** Changes should not be forced at once. They should be planned. People should get an opportunity to participate both in planning the change and installing it. This will help the group of the affected people to recognise the need for change and thus prepare themselves for receiving it without any fear. The time, place and quantum of change should be determined and the mode of introduction of change should also be planned.

3. **Protection of the Interest of Employees:** Management should ensure that employees will be protected from economic loss in status or personal dignity. If these things are protected, the degree of resistance to change will be very low.

4. **Group Dynamics:** Group dynamics refers to the everchanging interactions and adjustments in the mutual perceptions and relationships among members of the groups. Such group interactions are the most powerful instruments which facilitate or inhibit adaptation to change. Adaptation is a team activity which requires conformity to the new group norms, criterion, traditions and work patterns and styles. If these could be positively introduced by the management and group-based techniques for introduction of change are adopted, the results are likely to be more successful and durable.

5. **Changes should be Slow in Parts:** The management should not introduce any change at once and abruptly. The management must create awareness of change and develop an ability to be introduced in parts. If possible, the results must be reviewed and if required, adjustments must be made in it. This will not overload the management with responsibility and the whole system of change can be introduced with tested results at each stage.

6. **Proper Training:** In order to bring firmness in the changed order, the concerned employees should be properly trained. They should be able to know new techniques and knowledge. The concerned employees should be given orientation training. The policy of positive motivation should be used.

7. **Sharing of Income:** The extra income desired from changes should not be taken away by the management only, but should be shared with all the employees.

5.4.5 Kurt Lewin's Force Field Analysis Change Model

- **Kurt Lewin's** force field analysis change model was designed to weigh the driving and restraining forces that affect change in organisations. The 'force field' can be described as two opposite forces working for and against change. In this illustration we'll learn how to analyse the force field.

Force Field Analysis Change Model

- Have you ever had that conversation with colleagues about where to dine for lunch? You and a few others want to try the new Thai place, but your co-worker Jeanie and a few others want to go to the same old sandwich shop you've been going to for years. Well, Kurt Lewin's force field analysis change model describes a similar situation.

5.5 Change Management in Information System Development and Implementation Projects

- Information system development and implementation projects often tend to end in failure. According to research conducted by Standish Group, as many as 40% of information system development and implementation projects fail to complete. Standish Group classifies the success in the realisation of information system development and implementation projects into three types:
  - Successful projects;
  - Failed projects;
  - Projects exceeding the set deadlines and budget frameworks.
- The majority of projects end in failure. In addition to successful and failed projects, a "successful" completion of project which, however, exceeds set deadlines and budget frameworks is a frequent occurrence. Many projects fail, or are considered as failed in a particular aspect, but the issue is to what extent failure can be tolerated for the project to be still regarded as successful. Fig. 5.4 illustrates that the majority of projects belong to the category of failures. Looking at 2009 data, one can see that as many as 44% information system development and implementation projects ended in failure. This amounts to almost half of all the projects included in the research. On the other hand, the proportion of successful projects amounts to 24%, equaling approximately one-quarter. The remaining "challenged" projects account for 32%. If we view this part of the chart from the positive side, we can say that 56% of projects are successful. It is a positive fact that the percentage of successful projects is increasing, which may be the result of the increasingly serious management of information system development and implementation projects, taking into consideration change and risk management.

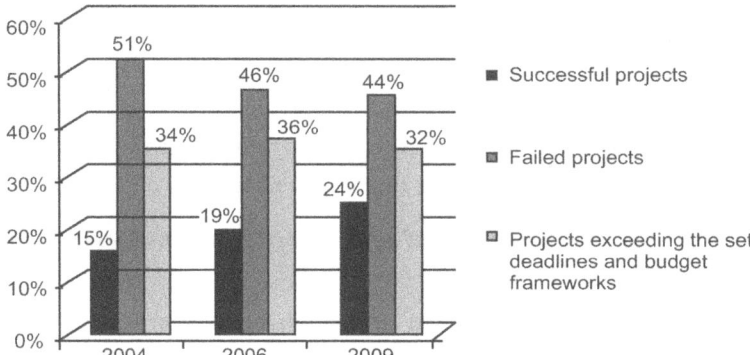

Fig. 5.4: Success rates of information system development projects

- As a complex process, managing information system development and implementation projects deserves a very high degree of attention. Project management in general, and especially IT-related project management, is virtually impossible without taking change into consideration. The process of change is a commonplace of contemporary business, and progress in inconceivable without change, because, as Rita Mae Brown would say, '[an excellent] definition of insanity is continuing to do the same thing over and over again, and expecting different results'. Changes, therefore, are inevitable, and should by no means be neglected in information system development and implementation projects. The next section of this article will deal in more detail with changes and possible ways of their successful implementation.

5.5.1 Change management

- As changes are difficult to predict, and tend to occur with growing frequency, change management is becoming an increasingly significant subject. Regardless of how a new information system is designed and how its implementation is planned, human potential represents a factor shat should play the key role in dealing with changes.
- Documented and functional change management is a decisive factor of project success, as changes are inevitable, especially in a complex, formative and evolving information system development project. James Taylor (2004) identifies two categories, i.e. types of changes:
    1. The first type refers to changes initiated by the client's need evaluation. These changes occur primarily because the requirements were not clear at the very beginning of the project, due to change of technology, or the change in needs caused by certain market requirements.

2. The second type refers to changes caused by the information system development and implementation project itself. These changes are often referred to as developmental changes. As developmental changes are mostly known in advance, it is necessary to find a way to monitor, i.e. control the change implementation itself. Lesley Partridge includes the following into the process of managing, i.e. controlling change implementation Fig. 5.5.
   - setting and managing objectives so that they are linked to the vision and purpose of change;
   - planning the details and required resources;
   - implementing the plan, with continuous monitoring;
   - possible adjustments of the plan or modification of actions based on information acquired by supervising change implementation, in order to ensure achievement of objectives or continue on the road towards them.

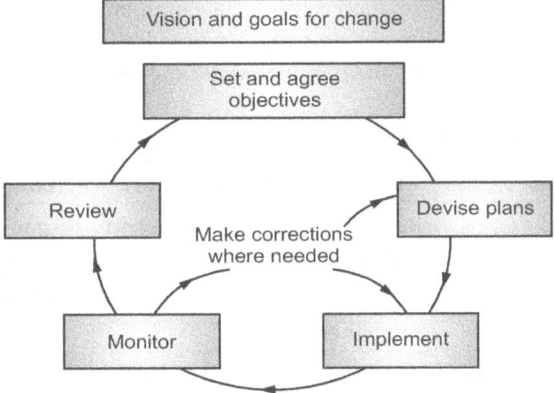

Fig. 5.5: Monitoring change implementation

5.5.2 Organisational changes

- Organisational changes condition the need for building a new information system. Cadle and Yates state four reasons for an organisation to invest in information system development:
    1. Business survival – in this context, time is frequently the key factor of success;
    2. Improving efficiency – in most cases, this means building a system that will provide high quality information required for decision support;
    3. Competitive advantage – rapid creation of prototypes and user solutions represent the strategies that are emphasised;

4. External factors – factors outside the organisation's control. It is necessary to avoid unpleasant surprises during the implementation stage, so it is necessary to devise a contingency plan.
- Cadle and Yates also identify the time and scope of the changes required as very important facts in managing information system development and implementation projects. Consequently, it is necessary to analyse the number of staff involved in the change process, how radically they have to adjust their attitudes and behaviour, as well as the time period available for implementing these changes.
- Table 1 shows the relationship between the length of the time period for change implementation and the type of change. A project bringing about radical changes over a brief period of time usually require changes of staff by way of employment. If the timescale is longer, and the changes are still extensive and far-reaching, it is necessary to re-engineer the business processes in order to secure the possibilities of the new system, Change Management in Information System Development and Implementation Projects Management Information Systems and sufficient time for upskilling of the existing staff. If the changes are incremental, their implementation implies providing a longer time period.

Table 5.3: Time and change matrix (Cadle & Yeates)

Change type	Short-term (3-9 months)	Long-term (1 year +)
Radical	Restructuring and redeployment of staff	Business process re-engineering
Incremental (gradual)	Process automation and refinement	TQM, innovation schemes

- When managing changes, it is essential to pay special attention to the following:
    - resistance to change
    - organisational culture
    - project participants, i.e. stakeholders

5.5.3 Resistance to change

- When developing and implementing an information system project, one frequently encounters resistance of the staff to the changes, because project managers did not foresee the staff's response to the changes occurring under the influence of the new system. Daryl Conner (as cited in Cadle & Yates, 2008) classifies the staff of an organisation into two types:
    - danger people (D-type) and
    - opportunity people (O-type)

- Project managers clearly belong in the O-type of people, because their job is actually to grasp new opportunities. On the other hand, the majority of new system users mostly belong in the D-type of people, because they see threats in these changes, and try to resist them.
- Another, similar staff classification, based on their impact on project progress (Cadle & Yates, 2008), includes:
    - promoters,
    - opponents,
    - latent opponents, and
    - potential promoters.
- Promoters have a positive attitude towards change in general, and implicitly, the specific changes brought about by the project. They see some personal benefits in these changes, or the possibility to use the advantages brought on by the changes. This category can be classified in the above mentioned O-type. Opponents are at the other extreme end, and they tend to have a negative attitude towards change in general, and take a negative view of the changes in the project. These two types of staff do not represent a problem; problems, however, may be caused by latent opponents and potential promoters. The latent opponents are the staff that may cause the greatest problems within a project. This group of people supports the changes, but only „on the surface", whereas potential promoters support change in general, but they need to be additionally convinced about the benefits of the changes brought about by the given project. Latent opponents tend to exercise passive resistance to change, for instance, they may agree to certain system functionalities, and then claim that the system is not doing what they want it to.
- Cadle and Yeates represent the changes over the project life cycle with the curve shown in Figure 3. The curve shown in the figure demonstrates early enthusiasm for the changes, which gradually declines as problems emerge, followed by 'gathering new strength' for facing the changes. Initially, the staff deny the new project because they feel challenged, and are consequently very sensitive regarding the development and implementation of the new project. At this stage, they are still convinced that they can apply the existing skills and knowledge to the new situation. Subsequently, as they learn more information about the project, they notice that the changes are greater than they expected, and begin to resist. As time passes, the staff diminish their resistance and increasingly want to solve the problems caused by the changes. Gradually, users cope with the challenges through discussions with colleagues and designers, or searching for errors within the designed system.

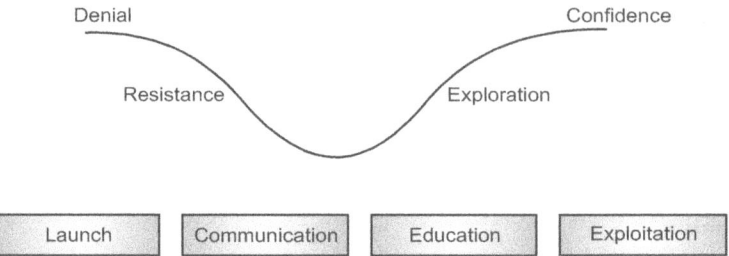

Fig. 5.6: The stages of change

5.5.4 Organisational Culture

- When planning change management in an information system development and implementation project, due consideration should be devoted to the culture of the organisation where the system is introduced. If the type of Zoran Ćirić, Lazar Raković 26 Management Information Systems organisational culture is established properly, it is much easier to develop tactics for overcoming resistance to change. Charles Handy classifies organisations in terms of centralisation and formality levels in business operations, into:
    - **Power cultures:** Organisations managed personally by owners often belong in this type, although larger organisations may also develop this type of corporate culture. In these organisations, the key issue is to gain explicit support of top managers, otherwise the staff will not co-operate. At this point, one should not ignore the fact that, regardless of all the formal paths through which the system is designed, nothing will be done unless it is approved by the top management.
    - **Task cultures:** In an organisation with taskbased culture, tasks are delegated to the lowest level, but the formal frameworks for reporting and decision-making have not been abolished. These organisations use task-based groups or teams in their operation. These organisations are said to have the most suitable culture for information system development and implementation projects, because disciplines such as planning, supervision and team-based responsibility are already incorporated in the organisational culture.
    - **Bureaucratic, i.e. role cultures:** The culture of these organisations is formal and centralised. All staff members have their roles, job descriptions and formal relations with other associated roles. In addition to formal relationships, one should not disregard the informal relationships among the staff either. If the project manager identifies informal relationships and uses some key contacts, he/she can obtain information and opinions much faster than through formal channels.

- o **Individualistic, i.e. person cultures:** An organisation with individualistic culture is informal and decentralised. These organisations are points of challenge in building information systems. Formal mechanisms, such as presentation, specification of project plans etc. are very scarce.
- It is, therefore, essential to determine the type of culture in which the organisation where the information system is implemented belongs. Based on this, it is much easier to predict customer behaviour, and the staff's possible reactions to change.

Project participants, i.e. stakeholders

- Participants in a project are of key importance for the success of change management in information system development and implementation projects. The role of individuals in the project is, therefore, highly significant. It is essential for all project participants what the scope of their task includes and what they should do. Otherwise, they will try to do everything they consider to be appropriate, but will probably not complete their tasks. Project participants include:
  - o project managers
  - o project sponsors
  - o team members
  - o change control board
  - o project managers
  - o **Project managers** are responsible for successful execution of the development and implementation of the project itself. They should supervise the complete project execution, and assist project participants. Project managers should identify the agents of change in an organisation, and to secure their involvement in the project. Project managers have a large volume of tasks, and are therefore forced to develop a plan of activities.
  - o **Project sponsors:** Project sponsors finance the execution of the project and must be certain that the project corresponds to the vision that they are trying to accomplish. They must also be certain that buildinga new information system will help accomplish the set organisational strategic objectives. Sponsors very often supervise the progress of the project, to make sure that it is realised in time and within the agreed budget.
  - o **Team members:** Team members are very important project participants. It is essential for the project manager to clearly present the tasks and objectives set before a particular team. It is, of course, important for the team members to understand what their specific tasks are.

- o **Change control board:** A change control board must be constituted in cases when the project is strategically critical, the scope of the project exceeds a few departments, etc. Basically, this board's role is to make strategic decision in terms of whether the project team should adopt certain changes or not. The change control board should include managers whose operation is influenced by the impact of the project.
- Cadle and Yeates (2008) state that people involved in a project should be classified according to the competence/commitment matrix (Fig. 5.7). People are classified in accordance with their competences (ability to create changes, implement them and cope with the process of change), and their commitment (belief in the need for change and their demonstration of this belief). People with high competence and low commitment can play a significant role in the change management process, but for some reason they are not willing to do it, or feel insecure about the changes. This situation needs to be examined and causes of low commitment have to be removed. The upper right hand cell of the matrix includes people who are able, willing and confident. They are often leaders of change and can make a positive impact on project development. The worst combination is if people are unwilling and unable to face the changes. This group has to be removed from the project. People placed in the lower right-hand cell are keen and motivated, but lack competence to lead or implement changes. These people need to be trained, and provided with adequate support and supervision.

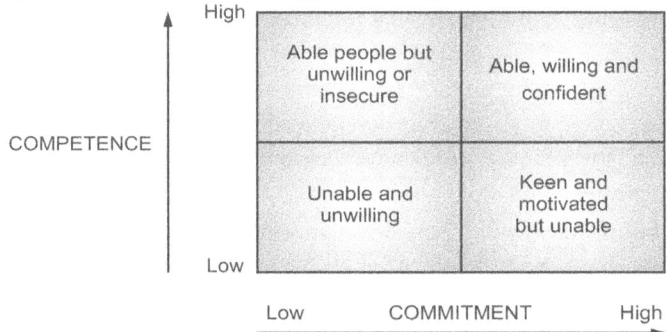

Fig. 5.7: Change competence/commitment matrix

Conclusion
- In information system development and implementation projects, it is vital to take change into consideration. In addition to change, it is essential to try and foresee the response of staff and team members to change, and try to manage it. In order to

facilitate predicting the staff's response to change, it is very important to determine initially the type of organisation where the system is implemented. Staff in organisations with different cultures and organisation schemes may respond to change in completely different ways. Therefore, change management, together with risk management and different information system development and implementation methodologies, can play a very significant role in successful project realisation. Of course, when managing change, it is not necessary to resort to extremes such as total resistance to change, or adoption of all proposed changes. Changes are necessary and must be managed if the objective is devising an information system that will meet the functional, time and budget frameworks set at the beginning.

■■■

University Question Papers
April 2015

Time : 3 Hours   Max. Marks: 80

Q.1 What are the types of computer memory? Explain in detail.   [15]
Ans. Refer to Section 1.3.

OR

Explain the types of computer in detail.
Ans. Refer to Section 1.1.6.

Q.2 What is DBMS? Explain database trends in short.   [15]
Ans. Refer to Sections 2.2.5 and 2.4.2.1, 2.5.

OR

What is traditional file environment? Enlist the problems in traditional file processing and compare traditional file system and DBMS.
Ans. Refer to Sections 2.4.5 and 2.4.

Q.3 Explain current trends in It management in detail.   [15]
Ans. Refer to Section 3.5.

OR

Explain different types of network topologies with diagrams in detail.
Ans. Refer to Section 3.4.

Q.4 What is World Wide Web? Explain its components.   [15]
Ans. Refer to Section 4.4.

OR

What is project? What is project management? Explain in detail its application in IT management.
Ans. Refer to Section 5.1.2.

Q.5 Write Short Notes on (any four):   [20]
(a) Management issues and decision.
Ans. Refer to Section 4.5.
(b) Change management.
Ans. Refer to Section 5.5.1.
(c) Use of social network in business.
Ans. Refer to Section 3.5.2.
(d) IT infrastructure for Digital firm.
Ans. Refer to Section 4.1.
(e) ICT applications.
Ans. Refer to Section 3.6.

IT in Management University Question Papers

November 2015

Time : 3 Hours Max. Marks: 80

Q.1 What is hardware and software? What are different types of application software? **[15]**
Ans. Refer to Sections 1.4.1 and 1.4.2.

OR

Draw block diagram of computer. What are functions of input and output devices? Explain any 3 input and output devices. Explain in detail.
Ans. Refer to Sections 1.1.5 and 1.4.2.

Q.2 What is DBMS? Explain different components of DBMS. **[15]**
Ans. Refer to Sections 2.2.5 and 2.2.6.

OR

Explain in detail different types of database models.
Ans. Refer to Section 2.4.2.1.

Q.3 Explain types of computer networks in detail. **[15]**
Ans. Refer to Section 3.3.

OR

Explain different types of network topologies with diagrams in detail.
Ans. Refer to Section 3.4.

Q.4 What is information system? Explain the challenges for managers in building information system. **[15]**
Ans. Refer to Sections 4.1 and 4.3.

OR

What is change management? Explain resistance to change and stages of change.
Ans. Refer to Section 5.5.1 and 5.4.4.

Q.5 Write short notes on (any four): **[20]**
  (a) Internet.
Ans. Refer to Section 3.1.
  (b) World Wide Web.
Ans. Refer to Section 4.4.
  (c) Project management.
Ans. Refer to Section 5.1.2.
  (d) Use of social network in business.
Ans. Refer to Section 3.5.6.
  (e) What is ICT?
Ans. Refer to Section 3.6.

www.ingramcontent.com/pod-product-compliance
Lightning Source LLC
Chambersburg PA
CBHW082232180426
43200CB00037B/2854